Christianity
9 to 5

Christianity

9 to 5

Living Your Faith at Work

MICHAEL A. ZIGARELLI

Beacon Hill Press of Kansas City
Kansas City, Missouri

Copyright 1998
by Beacon Hill Press of Kansas City

ISBN 083-411-7274

Printed in the
United States of America

Cover Design: Kevin Williamson

Library of Congress Cataloging-in-Publication Data
Zigarelli, Michael A.
   Christianity 9 to 5 : living your faith at work / Michael A. Zigarelli.
      p. cm.
   ISBN 0-8341-1727-4 (pbk.)
   1. Work—Religious aspects—Christianity.   2. Christian ethics.
I. Title.
BT738.5.Z54   1997
248.8'8—dc21   97-37907
                                                                     CIP

10   9   8   7   6   5   4   3   2   1

Sola Deo Gloria

CONTENTS

1

Stories from the Trenches

*A*FTER FOUR YEARS AT A CHRISTIAN COLLEGE *and months of job searching, the day had finally arrived. Mark had landed a job in a prestigious Big Six accounting firm and was ready to take on the world. He was sure to dress as his peers dressed, and he arrived early, hoping to make a good impression. Throughout the day he met dozens of new colleagues. He went to lunch with them and laughed at their jokes. He was careful to observe how people interacted, how they worked, and what was considered acceptable and unacceptable behavior. After his parents had invested so much to get him to this point, it was critical that he fit in so he could grow within this firm and make them proud.*

During the first few weeks, Mark was socialized into the company culture. He played on the company softball team, he stayed late with his colleagues to meet deadlines, and he occasionally went out with them after work. Mark was becoming one of the gang, and he found this comforting. Being new to this city, these were his first and closest friends.

As Mark's relationship with these people developed, conversations with them became more personal. Rather than simply involving the day's headlines or the firm's policy on sick leave, discussions began to center on how people felt about current events, political issues, and individuals within the firm. This seemed perfectly natural to Mark because this was exactly how his relationships back at school evolved. However, this time things were a little different. Mark was no longer insulated within a Christian culture. He was no longer surrounded by fellow Christians who shared his worldview and his love of the Lord. In fact, as best he could tell, many of his new friends seemed somewhat hostile to the perspectives he so tactfully kept buried inside of him. Mark decided that the best strategy under these conditions was to avoid such issues or, if they did come up, to simply bite his tongue. "Don't rock the boat," he thought to himself. "I've got a good thing going here, so just ignore this extraneous stuff."

9

Over time, though, this "stuff" didn't seem so extraneous. One friend made a habit of ridiculing evangelists. Another asked him to sign a pro-choice petition and attend a rally. A third was pilfering supplies from the firm on a daily basis. One of his female colleagues continually invited him to go out and have a drink with her. And then came the moment of truth. In the middle of what seemed to be an innocuous lunchtime conversation, one of Mark's colleagues asked him about his religious beliefs—the one topic Mark had been ducking for months as he built these relationships. After several months in the firm, he had established a rapport with these people and appeared to be on the fast track to management. Was he going to risk all that by letting out his deep, dark secret? What would people think? Would they still want to be his friends? And how would this affect his job and career?

Mark took a sip of water as the table grew silent.

If you're like most Christians, you probably have little difficulty relating to Mark's dilemma. You've probably encountered the same anxieties, experienced the same lack of courage, and struggled with the same uncertainty of how revealing your faith might alter your life at work. You may have even, after taking your sip of water, emphatically disavowed this critical dimension of your life just as Peter did 2,000 years ago! We all know this to be the safer road in the workplace, and it's a road with no shortage of Christian footprints.

But if you step back for a moment to put this in perspective, the decision to openly and actively express your faith at work should be an *easy* one. Think about it—your coworkers and your boss want you to act one way; the Creator of the universe wants you to act another way. So why do so few of us Christians confidently profess at work, through our words and actions, that we are believers?

The answer, of course, lies in the consequences of publicly owning our faith. Like Mark, we have achieved a comfort level with our peers at work. We may have earned a certain level of respect, a certain status. We may have a reputation to protect, a promotion to ensure, a pay raise around the corner. All of these things are in potential jeopardy when we acknowledge and apply our Christian faith at work. In fact, we *know* that some people, perhaps many people, are going to repudiate us and retaliate against us for living out our faith because Scripture says they will. When you live to please God, 1 John 3:13 tells us, "Do not be surprised . . . if the world hates you"!

Not a particularly comforting thought. Nobody wants to be hated at work—or anywhere else for that matter? But here's something that's infinitely more discomforting: if we instead choose to be friends with the world, that is, if we deny our Father in an effort to fit in, we become "an enemy of God" (James 4:4). So we find ourselves resolving on Sunday morning to take our chances with the world's hatred and to stand firm for Christ.

On paper and in church, that may be the obvious conclusion, but when the rubber actually hits the road Monday morning, things become increasingly complex. Consider for a moment the plight of these several Christian employees and employers who have paid a tremendous price to put God's Word into action in the workplace. Each is a true story of public record, and each offers some poignant insight into what can happen when we choose God's way on the job.

The Case of the "Religious Nut"

Sharing your faith will expose you to every sort of ridicule. You may be abused, called ugly names, lose the admiration of some of your peers, and you might even lose your job. Glenda knew the possible consequences but nonetheless elected to stand by her beliefs.

Glenda, like many Christians, believes that God is the most important part of her life. However, her employer made it clear to her her priorities were expected to be adjusted. During a training session, Glenda and the other trainees were told that their company had to be *the No. 1 priority in their lives.* Glenda initially shrugged this off as company propaganda but did feel a bit uneasy about the potential conflict.

Over time, Glenda courageously shared her faith with her coworkers, culminating somewhat predictably in accusations that she was a "religious nut" and a "religious hypocrite," and that she was "harassing her unit in a religious manner." She was also alleged to have placed religious pamphlets in the rest room. Her company investigated her behavior and documented her startling admission that her priorities were "God first, family second, and job third."

During the next several months, Glenda was subjected to harsh treatment that she believed was a direct result of her religious beliefs. She received an exceedingly low performance evaluation, she had repeated exchanges with a peer who labeled Glenda "Bible Bertha," and she was instructed by her new supervisor not to harass other employees about religion and not to proselytize on company property. Eventually, Glenda Beasley was fired, allegedly for poor work performance, thus ensuring that this "religious nut" would never again disrupt the company's work environment.[1]

The Case of the Persecuted Pro-Lifer

Christine Wilson, a Roman Catholic, worked as an information specialist for a very prominent company for 20 years. In July 1990, Christine took a religious vow to wear a two-inch button containing a color photograph of an 18-week-old unborn child "until there was an end to abortion." The button read, Stop Abortion, and They Are Forgetting Someone.

Some of Christine's coworkers asked her to remove the button, but Christine told them that she had made a promise to God to wear it at all times, except when sleeping or bathing. So offensive was this response, that some of Christine's coworkers protested by temporarily refusing to work. As a result, management claimed, office productivity declined approximately 40 percent during this time.

To resolve the problem, the company offered Christine three options: cover up the button, wear a different button with no photograph on it, or wear the button only when she was inside her cubicle. Christine responded that she could do none of these things because each option entailed compromising her promise to God to be a "living witness" by continually displaying this particular button. Soon thereafter, this 20-year veteran was terminated for the egregious offense of having three unexcused absences.[2]

The Case of the Christian Psycho

It's one thing to be ridiculed and ostracized for your beliefs; it's quite another to be sent for psychological help.

In all likelihood Ned was also amazed at the perplexing actions of his employer. Ned was a maintenance operator for approximately eight years. In 1987, he had an experience that led him to the conclusion that his primary goal in life was to serve God. Ned believed that the Lord wanted him to share his faith with a particular coworker. After much prayer and contemplating, Ned did witness to his friend. Subsequently, he was referred to the company's Employee Assistance Program. The function of the EAP was to help troubled employees overcome personal problems, whether they be alcoholism, marital problems, financial difficulties, or, apparently, religious convictions. Accordingly, the EAP counselor, after learning of Ned's witnessing, referred Ned to a psychiatrist! Ned, of course, knew that he did not need a psychiatrist but was nevertheless required to meet with one as a condition of continued employment. He kept the appointment, kept his job, and kept to himself thereafter.[3]

The Case of the Evangelizing Employer

Employers can be Christians too. In fact, when the boss practices biblically based management (see chapter 7), remarkable things can happen to employee morale and productivity. What's even more exciting is the potential for effective evangelism. Managers all over the world have actively witnessed to their subordinates, generating many converts. However, in the United States they have also succeeded in generating many lawsuits.

Warren Smith knows this all too well. Warren was the president of a manufacturer of electrical connectors. He founded the company in 1976 seeking to run a business for the Lord. To build a Christian company, Warren implemented business policies based on biblical principles and offered voluntary Bible study sessions to employees each week. In further pursuit of this goal, he also required managerial employees to attend an annual, weeklong training seminar on "basic life principles." This program, considered an invaluable management development tool by Warren, offered instruction in several areas, including conflict resolution in interpersonal relationships, dealing with anger, and responding to authority. The seminar was nondenominational but used references to Scripture to reinforce and illustrate its teachings.

One of the company managers attended two days of the

seminar and then, offended by its religious content, refused to attend the last three days. Warren was caught between what he believed the Lord wanted him to do in shaping his management team and what the manager claimed was nonwork-related proselytizing. He therefore sought a compromise by offering this person a transfer to a nonmanagerial position. In this way he could maintain the integrity of his training policy, and she could remain employed. What Warren received in response was a flat refusal, a subpoena to appear in court for violating the manager's civil rights, and significant disruption to his small business to defend the practice of his faith.[4]

The Case of Born-again Brown

Sharing your Christian faith can be especially treacherous if you work for the government. This is because some interest groups have succeeded in arguing that the U.S. Constitution's proscription on establishment of religion should be interpreted to mean that government is a religion-free zone. As a result, Christians who work in the public sector can be under tremendous pressure to keep their religious views to themselves. Some, like Isaiah, have refused to keep silent and have paid for it with their jobs.

Isaiah is a born-again Christian and was employed as the director of an information service in Iowa. For some time he was part of a group of county employees who met early in the morning for Bible study. After the county informed the group that such activities could not be tolerated on county property, the group began to meet elsewhere. However, Isaiah was later alleged to have permitted other employees to pray during department meetings in his office and, in one meeting, to have referred to Bible passages encouraging a strong work ethic.

This behavior was met with a stiff reprimand from his boss, who directed Isaiah to "cease any activities that could be considered proselytizing, witnessing, or counseling." He was to "ensure a work environment that is free of (these) types of activities." Moreover, the county demanded that Isaiah remove from his office all items that had any religious connotation, including a Bible that he kept on his desk. Reluctantly, Isaiah complied but was terminated soon thereafter for "lack of judgment" related to his handling of a budget.[5]

The Case of "Bible Bob"

Bob, after 37 years on a metropolitan police force, had risen from patrol officer to the department's second-in-command. He was also a devout Christian and faithful layperson at his church. Bob never concealed his convictions while on the job, and this decision earned him the unofficial titles of "Reverend Bob," "leader of the God squad," and "Bible Bob."

Eventually the city council caught wind of Bob's religious conviction and decided to investigate six police officers who gave sworn testimony that Bob never improperly injected his religious views into police department business and that they had been given promotions without inquiry into their personal convictions. Notwithstanding, later a council member introduced legislation that would prohibit any city employee from promoting his or her religious beliefs on the job.

Exhausted from this year-long ordeal and citing its damaging effect on his ability to worship, to participate in Christian fellowship, and to give public testimony to his faith, Bob announced his plans to retire. His distinguished career ended two months later.[6]

So What's Gotten into These People?

Clearly, our work lives would be less complicated if we Christians just kept our faith to ourselves. So why do people subject themselves to this kind of persecution? Isn't work hard enough without inviting the additional grief? Isn't the grind painful enough without inviting more suffering? What's gotten into these people anyway?

Plainly and simply, Jesus has.

Christ opened their eyes to the realization that work is more than a means to a paycheck. He opened their hearts to view work not just as something they do to put food on the table and a roof over their heads but also as a vehicle to serve Him. And He equipped them with the courage and fortitude to pursue their faith in the workplace, regardless of consequence. Simply put, Jesus asked these intrepid individuals to view work as a personal ministry, as a calling, and as a mechanism for modeling Christ to their neighbors.

However, this mission is not reserved for only a select few. Without exception, *every one of us is invited to serve Him in this way.* No matter what type of work you do, where you're employed, or how long you've been there, your work life can have a broader purpose than basic economics. Just like the individuals in the preceding stories, we can adopt the perspective of work as ministry and not worry whether or not our peers approve. All that matters is that God approves.

Each of these people came to the realization that first and foremost, *God is our real Boss.* Everything we do on the job is ultimately for the purpose of glorifying God, and the sooner we adopt this attitude, the sooner we will be able to effectively do His will in the workplace.

Scripture is replete with teachings on this very point. Probably the most widely quoted verse along these lines is Col. 3:23: "Whatever you do, work at it with all your heart, as working for the Lord, not for men." That's pretty direct. Here Paul is reminding the people of Colosse that because God is sovereign over everything, all of our work should be undertaken to honor Him. Paul visited this same theme with the Corinthians: "Whatever you do, do it all for the glory of God" (1 Cor. 10:31). Peter, too, addressed this point, writing, "If anyone serves, he should do it with the strength God provides, so that in all things God may be praised through Jesus Christ" (1 Pet. 4:11). In the workplace context, therefore, this all means that our service to the Lord is not suspended simply because we enter some building at 8 A.M. We're not temporarily exempt from serving because someone we work with might think we're a "religious nut." Instead, our real Boss asks us to continually "set [our] minds on things above, not on earthly things" (Col. 3:2) and, accordingly, to always be cognizant that we work for Him first.

This Boss Pays Well

So Bob, Glenda, and Isaiah said yes to God when He asked them to be living witnesses on the job. Warren said yes to God and trained his managers using biblical principles, and Ned did his best to be an effective Christian witness. These and countless others who have given their lives to Christ have endured the trials and persecutions inherent in becoming living sacrifices. And my guess is that if you were to ask them if they would do it all over again, there would be no hesitation in their affirmative responses. That's because no matter what the cost, working in recognition that God is your Boss has rewards that dwarf any monetary compensation, any promotion, any career path, or any title that could be conferred upon you here on earth. These stalwarts paid a significant price for acting on their convictions, but in doing so they stored up treasures in heaven. The reward is eternal!

Has the Lord ever asked you to apply your faith on the job? Has He ever spoken to you about a coworker or a customer? Has He ever tapped you on the shoulder when you pocketed those notepads? Has He ever asked you to take a stand at work on His behalf? If so, then you've probably already grappled with most of the issues dealt with in this book. You've likely struggled with the carnal versus the scriptural response to a difficult colleague. You've probably confronted inequitable pay, an unfair evaluation of your performance, or being passed over for a promotion. You've no doubt battled times of laziness, job dissatisfaction, and low productivity. In these respects, you're not uncommon. But you are called to be uncommon in your response to these and other such situations because you have the greatest Boss who ever walked the earth.

2

Coworker Conflicts

*M*ARK PUT DOWN HIS WATER GLASS *and glanced from one side of the table to the other. The moment had finally arrived—the one that several professors had advised him would inevitably occur in any secular workplace. He remembered shrugging off his mentors' prognostications. He remembered discounting the possibility that he would ever have any trepidation about sharing his faith. He even recalled smugly thinking that it was too bad that "lesser" Christians were so spineless.*

But now it was his vertebrae that were in question.

Perhaps it was divine intervention, perhaps it was that the sage advice of his parents and teachers had finally sunk in, but whatever the reason, Mark felt a surprising inner peace come over him, prompting the response: "Well, I'm a Christian. I've been saved since I was 12 years old."

The words just sort of fell out of his mouth. And as it always had, it felt liberating to say them. Emboldened by this feeling, he excitedly continued as if he were speaking with one of his friends back at school. "Since then I've considered Jesus my personal Savior. My Brother. My Friend. And in turn, He has blessed me in countless ways."

By this point, the expressions confronting Mark were not the familiar nods and assuring smiles he had seen before from like-minded peers. Quite the contrary, his comment met with everything from blank stares to eye rolling to head shaking. One colleague, John Taylor, was laughing.

"That's great stuff, Marko. And I'm a televangelist on the weekends. Did you know that just two dollars will save your soul?"

"He's serious, John," Barbara interrupted with a touch of attitude. "I don't believe it. We've actually got a full-fledged Bible thumper on our hands here."

"Oh stop it, Barb," returned John. "Don't insult my buddy that way. Mark, will you please inform Miss No-Sense-of-Humor that you're simply doing your best Billy Graham imitation?"

*Inner peace gave way to panic, but there was no escaping this now. "Uh . . . actually," Mark stuttered somewhat contritely, "she's right. I **was** serious."*

"Ha!" Barbara shrieked as John's jaw dropped.

*"You've got to be kidding," another colleague chimed in. "You **really** buy into that Jesus stuff?"*

"Come on, Mark," another said in a motherly tone and with a sad smile. "I know you're more enlightened than that."

"Marko, who's brainwashed you?"

"He's the one who wants to do the brainwashing, John," Barbara again interjected. "I suppose you're one of those anti-choice people too. Bomb any abortion clinics lately?"

Prominent on our long list of workplace challenges is dealing with coworker problems. It is with these people that we spend hundreds, even thousands of hours each year. With a few of them, we have perhaps enjoyed some of the best moments of our lives. However, for most of us anyway, other coworkers have been at the root of our most disturbing, most embarrassing, or most exasperating moments. During such times, we have struggled to identify and then to implement God's will.

This chapter will offer several biblically based suggestions for addressing coworker issues, giving particular attention to resolving conflicts with coworkers, avoiding workplace gossip, and handling personal attacks. Before we get into the specifics, though, it is important to start by examining *the primary obstacle* to Christlike behavior toward our coworkers. It is an invisible yet formidable enemy that tends to corrupt almost everyone at work. It's called the corporate culture.

The Influence of Corporate Culture

Think about the places you've worked in your life. Wasn't there a distinctive character to each one? Wasn't there an overall atmosphere resulting from things like the pace of work and the way in which people treated one another? Wasn't there some set of both written and unwritten guidelines regarding the parameters of appropriate conduct?

Every workplace has a corporate culture. Technically speaking, it is the collection of shared assumptions about how one should think and feel about various situations, including how one can and should interact with one's coworkers. Some job environments are very casual and sedate; others are intense and stressful. In some companies, coworkers tend to get along well and may even feel as though they are part of a family. In others, the cultural norm is hostility, suspicion, gossip, and complex office politics. In one workplace people may treat others with respect, but in the workplace next door they may not. The general tone of your work environment is a large part of what is meant by "corporate culture."

Although unseen, this culture is powerful. It has the power to control behavior. It has the power to change attitudes. It has the power to shape people into its own image—even the most committed Christians. It is seldom fully consistent with biblical principles and has too often encouraged us Christians to adopt its secular rules of the game when relating to our coworkers. *We therefore need to understand how our corporate culture influences us so that we may, if necessary, overcome it and maintain a Christlike attitude toward our coworkers and our jobs.*

Indoctrination into a corporate culture begins when we first sit in the interview chair. Increasingly, employers seek to hire people who not only have the required knowledge, skills, and abilities to do the job but also "fit" the environment. That is, an employer will often give tremendous weight to whether one's personality, communication style, values, work ethic, and attitude are compatible with those of people already employed at the company. An interviewer will thus explore our background and ask us questions that simultaneously solicit important information and signal to us how we will be expected to behave as an employee. An example might be, "Do you have any constraints that would prevent you from working long hours?" With such a question, the interviewer is both seeking vital data and sending a message about the job environment. This conversation affords us a first glimpse of the culture into which we are supposed to assimilate.

Once we have taken the new job, we are socialized to think and act as everyone else does. How we should behave is communicated to us *directly* through orientations, training programs, and mentoring, and, perhaps more potently, *indirectly* through the way our coworkers dress, the type of language they use, the way they associate with one another, the stories they tell about one another, and their willingness to respect the organization's stated rules and traditions. We learn through this socialization process both the boundaries of acceptable and unacceptable conduct and the largely unwritten directives for interacting with others in our new workplace. These behavioral norms are continually reinforced in our daily work lives.

This phenomenon poses a significant danger to Christians who work in environments whose cultural norm is not "love thy neighbor as thyself." We are at risk of undergoing a metamorphosis. We are in jeopardy of being converted into a gossip, a sniper, and a colleague who is inconsiderate, contentious, defensive, indifferent, or whatever else is most typical at work. The culture's rules become our rules, and God's rules take a backseat.

The apostle Paul warns us of this possibility in 1 Cor. 15:33 where he writes: "Bad company corrupts good character." Quite simply, there is a tendency to become like those with whom we associate. We can easily become products of our environment; therefore, we must actively guard against this transformation by vigilantly monitoring ourselves and resisting the daily pressures that may influence us away from Christlikeness. Each time a wave of culture hits us squarely in the face (for instance, when a coworker seeks to gossip about the boss or when a coworker advises us to retaliate against someone), we need to take immediate steps to avoid having our character corrupted.

One very effective technique for combating this pollution is to continually replace ungodly thoughts with godly ones. Each one of us is like a sponge. Typically, what we soak up is what ultimately comes out when we are squeezed. All day every day we are soaking up the behavior of others around us at work. And often it is not behavior that we should be emulating. When we are squeezed—when a situation arises that calls for some response on our part—unless we have wrung out the dirty water in the sponge and replaced it with clean water, it is the dirty water that others are likely to see. Our response will reflect the corporate cultural norm and, in many cases, be displeasing to God.

We can avoid this outcome by making a habit of resisting the corrupting influence of corporate culture. This sounds like a time-consuming and arduous task, but in fact, it's relatively simple. Phil. 4:8 provides the antidote to succumbing to the work environment:

Whatever is true, whatever is noble, whatever is right, whatever is pure, whatever is lovely, whatever is admirable—if anything is excellent or praiseworthy—think about such things.

Paul is telling us here to fix our eyes on Christ and to fill our minds with His teachings and thoughts of His sacrifice for us. These are the things that are true, noble, right, pure, and so on. In the context of the workplace, an effective way to avoid being dirty sponges, then, is to simply flood the sponge with clean water. That is, *we can overcome the corrupting influence of corporate culture by inundating ourselves on the job with reminders of our faith.* Read the Bible when you can at work. Pray often. Listen to a Christian radio station, if possible. Think about last Sunday's sermon. Let hymns of praise reverberate through your brain in place of whatever other tune is presently there. By doing so, you are, in effect, insulating yourself by putting on the armor of God. And this is a shield that even the strongest corporate culture cannot penetrate.

Resolving Conflicts God's Way

But no matter how proficiently we swim against the current of corporate culture and no matter how Christlike our behavior, we're still going to run into friction with people on the job. The workplace is permeated with ambition, pride, envy, arrogance, greed, and a myriad of other sins. It is also the world's most fertile breeding ground for gossip and slander. In almost any job, we'll meet individuals with exceedingly abrasive personalities and others who are simply perpetual complainers. Occasionally, we encounter coworkers who, for whatever reason, seek to undermine us by criticizing or even taking credit for our good work. Extra effort on our part is seldom repaid with a thank-you or any type of meaningful reward, and it seems that just when we are spread as thinly as we can be, higher-ups then ask for more. In such an environment, conflict with those around us is inevitable.

So how can we deal with this? Many people have tapped the voluminous secular advice on conflict resolution. Literally hundreds of books, some of which are pretty good, have been published to advance some new strategy for resolving our problems with other people or with powerful institutions. Phrases such as "alternative dispute resolution," "mediation and conciliation," "negotiating to win," "mutual gains bargaining," and "win-win solutions" are now a common part of the American lexicon, especially in the workplace. In fact, our unquenchable thirst for negotiating and dispute resolution advice has propelled books such as *How to Argue and Win Every Time*,[1] *Getting to Yes: Negotiating Agreement Without Giving In*,[2] and *Negotiating for Dummies*,[3] among others, to the top of best-seller lists. Clearly, one available option for managing our workplace conflicts is to read up on the latest panacea.

However, we must be wary. The common thread through many of these popular resources is that each purports to help us meet our needs, our "bargaining objectives," without giving up too much. This is the epicenter of secular conflict resolution theory. You want something from someone and here is a way for you to get it. Your rights are in jeopardy, and this resource will tell you how to efficiently secure them. Timeless problems, contrived solutions.

Fortunately, and this will come as no surprise, we do not need to rely on such solutions because the Lord has a conflict resolution approach of His own. The Bible advises us what to do before, during, and after every conflict. Its components are as follows:

Before the Conflict: Adopt a Servant's Mind-set Toward Coworkers

I once had a cantankerous colleague named Jake who always seemed to think the world was out to get him. Over the years I worked with him he made some of the most callous comments I've heard from anyone in the workplace. Once I told Jake that a coworker of ours was recently involved in a car accident and was now in the hospital. Jake gruffly replied, "Why should I care about him, about you, or, for that matter, about anyone else around here!"

That's pretty harsh stuff. But, while few of us have ever combined such words into one sentence, Jake's question does, it seems, summarize the attitude that many people, including some Christians, have toward those with whom they work. For many of us, there is a little Jake buried deep down inside, whose thoughts never make it past our larynx, but who nonetheless still shapes our demeanor and our actions toward our coworkers. We perhaps do not like our coworkers very much. We may find them to be irritants or inhibitors to our productivity. We may find their personalities, lifestyles, or work habits to be bothersome or offensive. As a result, Jake is spawned and begins to grow. And before we know it, he is dominating our conduct toward almost everyone at work.

Contrast this to the relationship that Christ had with those around Him. Christ came, not to condemn others, not to be waited on by others, not to operate independently of others, but to be a servant. He washed people's feet, He healed the sick, He taught, He prayed for people, and He carried and relieved their burdens. Whatever people asked of Him, He did. And in doing so, He modeled for us the perspective we Christians should adopt toward our coworkers and everyone else: *As servants of Christ, we exist to serve others and to meet their needs before we meet our own.*

We see this truth revealed not just in the person of Christ but throughout Scripture. A tandem of verses, I think, illustrates this exceptionally well. Many people are familiar with John 3:16, which says that God loved us so much that He sent His Son to die for our sins. Fewer, though, have memorized the corollary to this, 1 John 3:16, which says that just as Christ laid down His life for us, "we ought to lay down our lives for our brothers." We are to serve them however we can, whenever we can, as well as we can. This, of course, includes those at our workplace.

In large part, the extent to which we are willing to forgo our needs to meet the needs of others is a measure of our maturity in the Christian faith. It is a gauge of our spiritual formation. In the workplace, then, the mature Christian always permits the interests of others to supersede his or her own. When they need assistance, he or she is the first to render it. When they have a complaint, he or she tries to resolve the problem. When they have a deadline, the Christian helps meet it even if it is not his or her responsibility. The Christian's own interests, needs, and ambitions are subordinate to those of coworkers. Both off and on the job, servanthood is to be a defining characteristic of our lives.

This is a completely different paradigm from that to which

we are accustomed at work. It is the antithesis of Jake. Instead of thinking, "What are my needs?" or "What can this person do for me?" and instead of considering ourselves at odds with our coworkers, our first thought whenever we see a coworker is always, "What does this person need, what's weighing on this person's mind, and what can I do to help?" Once we can make this adjustment, besides making a few more friends, two extraordinary things happen.

First, we'll be much happier at work. People who are dissatisfied with their jobs most often feel this way because they perceive that their needs are not being met. Whether it is their need to have challenging work, to receive a pat on the back, to get things done as efficiently as possible, to gain complete economic security, or to have any number of other things, many jobs and job environments come up short. Like others around us, we incessantly focus on the fact that our jobs, our bosses, and our workplaces do not satisfy these needs, and we become disappointed, aggravated, and even enraged at times. The fault may lie in our own selfishness, in others' failings, in the corporate culture, or in all of the above, but regardless the culprit, the fact remains that we perpetually wear the chains of discontent. It has enslaved us at work and probably far beyond.

By contrast, people who focus on meeting the needs of others without regard for their own needs have little to anger them at work. We all know people like this. They're always whistling some tune, wearing a smile, apparently under little stress, and willing to lend a hand. The expression on their face says, "What can I do for you?" They have a servant's mentality, little self-interest, and fewer expectations, and as a direct result, they are much more satisfied with their work environment than they would be otherwise.

A second important consequence of servanthood is that we will find ourselves in fewer conflicts with our coworkers. Because conflicts most often occur in the workplace when people attempt to advance competing needs or interests, shifting one's focus to the needs of others will minimize the chance that competing interests will exist in the first place. Servanthood is, therefore, an extremely effective foundation for workplace dispute resolution, because in most cases, it stops a conflict before one ever starts.

During the Conflict: Focus on the One Important Question

Some conflict with coworkers will occur, though. Even Christ himself, the perfect Model of servanthood, found himself embroiled in several conflicts during His ministry. When workplace disputes arise, rather than first turning to secular best-sellers, we can turn for instruction to the best-selling Book of all time.

Let's say that you believe you're clearly the next in line for a promotion. As sometimes happens, though, you are passed over for someone else. Now let's say that this happens twice more. You have a problem. You're doing good work, you've been around longer than those to whom you are now reporting, and you could really use the money that the higher position entails. Your servant's attitude has prevented you from storming into anyone's office or getting in anyone's face about the issue. You've tried to de-emphasize your needs and have only subtly expressed your concern by simply dropping hints that you would be very interested in the next available promotion.

Now, after being overlooked for a third time, there is no denying that you feel wronged, cheated, even exploited. The questions that permeate your mind whenever you think about this situation (and that is often) are, "What are my rights here?" "Who's at fault for my predicament?" and "What can I do to ensure that I'm the one promoted the next time?" It's human nature to think this way when one feels mistreated.

But are these the questions God wants us to ask in such a situation? In the midst of workplace conflict, is it on rights, blame, and personal fulfillment that He wants us to focus our attention and our energy? When we have a dispute with our superiors, our peers, or our subordinates, isn't there some other question we should be asking instead? Ray Stedman, the late pastor and best-selling author, draws on Ephesians to offer some incisive advice.[4]

Paul, in this letter, deals very candidly with many delicate subjects: lying, stealing, gossiping, hatefulness, and sexual misconduct, among others. In the fifth and sixth chapters he takes up the issue of personal relationships. Stedman notes that through Paul's counsel to wives, husbands, parents, children, slaves, and masters, we see a very interesting pattern develop—

one that will assist us in resolving the promotion problem. Paul writes:

- "Wives, submit yourselves to your husbands, as to the Lord" (5:22).
- "Husbands, love your wives, just as Christ loved the church" (5:25).
- "Children, obey your parents in the Lord" (6:1).
- "Fathers, do not exasperate your children; instead, bring them up in the training and instruction of the Lord" (6:4).
- "Slaves, obey your earthly masters . . . just as you would obey Christ" (6:5).
- "And masters, treat your slaves in the same way. . . . since you know that he who is both their Master and yours is in heaven" (6:9).

Notice that in each of these passages, Paul makes reference to not only the two people in the relationship but also the Lord, His authority, and His universal presence. He is communicating here a fundamental Christian principle that there is no such thing as a strictly two-person relationship. No matter what type of relationship we find ourselves in—spousal, parental, employment, friendship, stranger, whatever—we must remember that we are never alone with this person. It is never just one-on-one. We are not the only parties concerned. *There is always a third party, Christ himself, present with the two of us.*

Applying this truth to the promotion issue (or any conflict), it is likely that the Lord wants us to take a different approach from what seems most natural. In the midst of conflict, our first responsibility is to remind ourselves that Christ is standing in the doorway. He is the neutral Mediator of this dispute, and He hears all and knows all. It may appear that we must deal with only one person—our boss—over the promotion, but Christ is part of this relationship too. When we remain cognizant of this, our focus changes from securing rights and independently fulfilling our needs to pleasing the Lord. We de-emphasize the justice aspect, refrain from the assignment of blame, disregard what we personally want the resolution to be, and instead concentrate on what the Mediator has to say. In other words, we approach this problem and every conflict by contemplating on the *only* relevant inquiry here: "What does Christ want me to do in this situation?"

In the specific case of being passed over for promotion, this does not necessarily mean that you say nothing, go on getting passed over, pretend nothing is wrong, and shrug your shoulders saying, "Oh well, God has a plan here." It *may* mean that, as we'll discuss in greater detail in chapter 5, but Christ may prompt you to do something else. Ask Him what He wants you to do. Give Him your complete attention and let Him respond. Then, vigorously pursue His will. One thing is for sure: He will not encourage you to do anything that is contrary to His teachings. He will help you avoid the un-Christlike response that is so often our first impulse in such disputes. He will mediate your dispute, if you will let Him, and although you may not be immediately satisfied with the resolution, His wisdom will reveal itself over time.

When entangled in a workplace dispute, step back and seek the answer to the one important question.

After the Conflict: Stand Firm in the Face of Criticism

And what of the aftermath? Some coworkers will attempt to tell you that you are being foolish for adopting this approach to resolving disputes. They may tell you that you did not get what you deserved, that you've been manipulated, that you look weak, or that you're incompetent. And isn't there some merit to their conclusions? After all, would you be able to get more from your boss, peer, or subordinate by using a different dispute resolution approach? Probably. Will you be exploited? Occasionally. Will others perceive you as ineffective because of your concessions? Perhaps. Sometimes the critics can be so harsh and their reasoning so deceptively compelling that it appears rational to abandon Christ's model.

But like the questions "What are my rights?" and "Who's at fault?" your coworkers' questions are also irrelevant. There is but *one* pertinent consideration when the smoke clears: *Would God say to you, "Well done"?* If the answer to that question is yes, the answers to the other questions do not matter. People may scoff at your approach when you adopt God's model of conflict resolution, but remember Paul's words to the Corinthian church: "The foolishness of God is wiser than man's wisdom, and the weakness of God is stronger than man's strength" (1 Cor. 1:25).

So do not acquiesce. Stand your ground after the conflict has been resolved. They may regard you as foolish and weak, but once you are satisfied that you have done God's will, do not be persuaded to reopen the discussion to get what others might think you rightfully deserve. Trust the Lord enough to use the dispute resolution tools He has provided and to embrace the solution that He has brokered. Be a servant in all your relationships, remain focused on what Christ wants you to do during the conflict, and disregard the world's inevitable criticisms of the outcome.

Advice for Dealing with the Especially Difficult Coworker

Before leaving the subject of conflict resolution, one final predicament needs to be addressed: dealing with the "impossible" coworker. This person is a rare breed that we encounter in some workplaces. When we do encounter them, though, we usually wish we hadn't. I'm talking about the person who has made your work life so arduous that the distraction has carried over into your home, the person whose words and actions have caused you to lose sleep, the person who has wronged you time and again and actually seems to enjoy it. It can be a boss or a peer, but regardless, nothing you have said or done—including servanthood and forgoing self-interest—has alleviated the problem.

It is possible that the situation will never be resolved. However, there is one nifty technique that may be worthwhile to try because it often results in at least some relief. I do not know to whom it is originally attributed, but I have little doubt that the inventor was an accomplished student of human relationships. The technique is called the 101 Percent Principle.

This approach to dealing with an especially difficult person says that we should find the 1 percent of things on which we agree with this person, and devote 100 percent of our energy to this commonality when we are with them (hence, 101 percent). That is, we should, if possible, *only* talk with them about whatever minuscule intersection of opinion or interest we have and *never or seldom* discuss the many things on which we disagree. In theory, by focusing all of our time with this person on some common bond, the nature of our relationship should change. We will begin to drain at least some of whatever is leading our nemesis to give us such a hard time. Eventually, he or she may come to view us as not so bad after all, or even as one of the "good guys."

Of course, this is much easier to read than it is to do. A co-worker who is abusing, harassing, or persecuting you is not someone with whom you want to discuss *anything*. But sometimes, because of the proximity of this person or because of the interdependence of your jobs, you will not be able to avoid him or her. In conjunction with the forgiveness tenets discussed later in this chapter, the 101 Percent Principle may relieve an intense, exacting situation and may thereby yield a better night's sleep.

Workplace Gossip

Work at any job for even a short period of time and you're guaranteed to be exposed to gossip. Coworkers talk about each other—a lot. And much of the time the discussion goes well beyond the simple sharing of neutral information about what happened when to whom. In many of our workplace conversations, we hear subjective, negative evaluations of coworkers who are not a part of the discussion. Then, we often see others in the conversation pile on, escalating the attack. It happens several, perhaps dozens, of times each workday in almost every job. Should this be of any concern to us as Christians? Do we have any responsibility to avoid or restrain such behavior?

To answer these questions, let's start with a definition. *Gossip,* as I am using the term here, simply means discrediting talk about someone who is not present. We gossip for many reasons, one of which is to seek revenge. We may feel wronged by individuals, and rather than directly confronting or ridiculing them, we elect to malign them and to spread rumors about them behind their backs. Gossip also exists to bond people who are engaging in it. Talking about a common enemy or problem brings us closer together. Additionally, gossip cements the corporate culture. Because gossip tends to identify personal traits and behaviors that people find disagreeable, it functions as a reinforcement mechanism for the social norms of the workplace. For example, a discussion between two people that criticizes another coworker for dressing poorly is gossip that not only disparages that coworker but also reinforces the norm that one should dress professionally, or at least neatly, in that work environment.

A final reason that people find workplace gossip especially appealing is something that makes it especially sinful: we often gossip to knock someone down a few notches so that we may then look and feel superior to him or her. We try to enhance our image at the expense of someone else's. And in many cases, we do not even consciously realize that this is why we are gossiping! But think about it—isn't this one of the major reasons why those trashy television talk shows attract so many viewers? Don't people who are watching marvel at the deviance or absurdity of the guests and then somehow consider themselves better because they would never descend to that level? Don't these shows bolster our own self-image by degrading the lives and actions of others? Workplace gossip serves the same purpose. One rationale for criticizing someone's wardrobe may be to highlight our own.

Gossip, then, is clearly not something in which we should engage, because when we do we score big on the sinfulness index—slander and pride in one brief conversation (and perhaps a little vengeance or even envy thrown in for good measure). Furthermore, Scripture speaks explicitly to the issue of gossip in many places without equivocating: gossiping is a sin (e.g., Rom. 1:29; 2 Cor. 12:20). One who gossips "betrays a confidence" (Prov. 20:19), "separates close friends" (Prov. 16:28), and is always "saying things [he or she] ought not to" (1 Tim. 5:13). Therefore, we must abstain from gossiping. Period. And when we do so, we are not only remaining in God's will but also receiving an added windfall related to the conflict resolution model discussed above. Prov. 26:20 says, "Without wood a fire goes out; without gossip a quarrel dies down." Less gossip equals fewer conflicts.

Since we indeed have a responsibility to avoid gossip, what are we to do in a work environment that is saturated with it? Is there any way to really stifle it in our workplace conversations? Believe it or not, a substantial amount of gossip research has been conducted by sociologists, psychologists, and anthropologists. They have examined everything from what gossip is to why it exists to the role it plays in society. Most importantly for our purposes here, some very good research has also been conducted on how gossip progresses and how a participant in a conversation can effectively cut it off.

In analyzing the structure of gossip, researchers at the University of Indiana, in perhaps the best empirical study of its kind, found that when someone in a group conversation expresses a negative opinion about an individual who is not present (i.e., when gossip first begins), *the first response from the group to this opinion will often determine whether or not more gossiping will occur in that conversation.*[5] More specifically, if the first response to this negative statement supports the comment, then the gossiping tends to spiral. Other people in the conversation consider it safe to agree (and unsafe to disagree) with the opinion, and it typically becomes open season on the target of the gossip. However, if the first response to the negative comment is a challenge to it (i.e., if someone immediately disagrees with or questions the assessment before anyone else endorses it), then the conversation is much less likely to become a gossipfest. Often, the initial speaker responds by moderating or even retracting the opinion, and the conversation goes in any number of directions. People in the conversation feel free to either agree or disagree with the initial evaluation, because they know they will not stand alone.

Also noteworthy, the researchers found that if the initial negative comment is immediately seconded by another person in the conversation, it is much more difficult for someone else to then challenge the negative evaluation in an attempt to head off the gossip. This is because once someone has agreed with the first speaker, anyone desiring to challenge the initial comment must take on at least two people and maybe the whole group. By contrast, when one takes issue with a negative comment before it has been seconded, that person is, at that point, challenging only one individual's evaluation. This is significantly less risky, especially in a work environment.

These research conclusions, it seems, make intuitive sense. We've all been in such conversations, and we've seen them either intensify or wither based on the first response. Moreover, this is also valuable information for Christians because it demonstrates how we can put some reins on workplace gossip. Anytime gossip rears its ugly head, we should immediately, but gently, challenge it. We should respond with a counteropinion or raise some doubt before the comment is ever endorsed. And in those cases where we actually agree with the negative assessment, rather than joining in or even remaining silent, we can look for a creative way to quickly steer the conversation elsewhere. In other words, we neither endorse nor denounce the negative opinion but instead tactfully change the subject.

You'll no doubt have ample opportunity to try this technique, so experiment with it. Learn how to diplomatically extinguish gossip as soon as it begins. When you make this a habit, you will find yourself not only participating in much less gossip at work but also further reducing conflicts with and among your coworkers.

Attacks on You and Your Faith

Mark, our friend from the accounting firm, stuck out his neck and had his head chopped off. As we saw from the anecdotes in chapter 1, it happens to Marks nationwide every day. We are ridiculed by our coworkers for adhering to principle, for refusing to work on the Sabbath, for seeking to spread the gospel at work, and for our supposedly intolerant agenda.

Contemporary corporate cultures discourage almost every form of individual harassment, but harassment of those professing to be committed Christians is still permissible. And the problem is getting worse, as indicated by a recent federal government attempt to institutionalize workplace assaults on Christians. In 1994, the Equal Employment Opportunity Commission, the federal administrative agency charged with enforcing most employment discrimination laws, sought to define "religious harassment" to mean any expression of one's faith in the workplace that a coworker could construe as offensive. The only way that employers could ensure that they would not run afoul of the new law would be to maintain a completely religion-free workplace—no more Bibles on desks, no more religious calendars or pictures in one's work space, no more religious jewelry or T-shirts, and certainly no more evangelizing.

Although this sweeping redefinition of religious harassment has to date never been adopted as law, its proposal is a striking bellwether of what Christians face in the secular workplace. But get used to it. When you speak and live God's truth on the job, workplace trials are inescapable. The question that must occupy us, then, is: How do we respond appropriately?

As believers, we are called to deal with these trials as Christ would, and that means going well beyond ignoring or "tolerating" those who encumber us. We Christians have a broader responsibility and one that requires tremendous fortitude. The Lord instructs us to *forgive* our persecutors.

For most of us, this is troubling. Christians who have suffered in this way and have grappled with the alternative responses to such attacks, regardless of where they are in their walk with Christ, know how wrenching this command can be. The mere *thought* of forgiving those who've hurt us engenders anguish and consternation. In such situations, we try to suppress the notion of forgiveness, to run from it, or to conveniently ignore it. Sometimes, we rationalize that God couldn't have intended the principle of forgiveness to apply to such egregious circumstances. But like Adam and like Jonah, we soon find that there is no place one can hide from God and His truth. We are therefore compelled to contemplate the seemingly extreme option of forgiveness.

Try Something Radical: Forgive Them

When people at work ridicule us; when they gossip and tell lies about us; when they chastise us for our religious convictions; when they laugh at us or ostracize us, there is nothing we want to do less than forgive them. Rather, most people, including Christians, select one of two alternatives in response.

First, some of us elect to fight. We may report their behavior to higher management, attempt to embarrass them in front of other coworkers, or file a lawsuit—somehow try to make them pay for what they did to us. We surrender to our instincts, make a lifetime enemy, and mar the cause of Christ.

Others of us, and probably the majority of us, choose a second option: flight. If people are bugging us, we get away from them. We get a transfer to another department or maybe even quit our job to find another one. We simply attempt to escape the situation altogether. This clearly is a superior response to striking back at them, but it is similarly inadequate. Regardless of where we go, whether it is to another job in the same organization or to some other employer, our beliefs will draw the derision of some people. *The Bible guarantees that we will encounter opposition.* John 15:19, among other verses, tells us that we will be strangers in this world. Our estrangement is by design, so fleeing a hostile job environment, in many cases, will afford us only temporary relief from rebuke.

We are left, therefore, with only one permanent solution, one viable choice, one path to lasting peace. We are left with God's alternative: forgiveness.

Forgiveness is restoring someone back to his or her original condition. It means to refuse to remember the wrong of the perpetrator, to give up our right to be mad at this person, and to completely clear the slate. Jesus' parable in Matt. 18 about the forgiving master and the unforgiving servant is a fundamental and plain illustration that forgiveness is not just another option; it's a duty that goes to the very core of our faith.

We are further instructed by this same passage of the Gospel that forgiveness is to be a habit, a lifestyle. We are to forgive as many times as someone wrongs us, without remembering just how often it has been. This means that the majority of us who seem to keep a mental scorecard of forgiveness frequencies are not really forgiving at all, because we're not refusing to remember what this person has done. As often as the Master forgives us, so, too, must we servants forgive one another.

Unforgiveness and Its Consequences

Even though forgiveness is the centerpiece of the Christian faith, and even though our salvation is impossible without God's forgiveness, it is the domain where Christians have a great deal of difficulty. We offer dozens of reasons for refusing to forgive, but among the most commonplace, it seems, are the following:

- The persons who hurt us do not deserve our forgiveness.

- We have a right to be mad and a right to punish these persons by not forgiving them.

- If we forgive them, they won't even know they've wronged us, and they'll simply continue this behavior.

- We dislike these persons and deep down do not want this to change. Unforgiveness insulates us from discovering any redeeming characteristics in them.

- We enjoy the role of martyr because it allows us to show the world how tough we have it. Rather than forgive, through complaining and gossip we continually communicate that we've been wronged.

This unwillingness to forgive our coworkers distances us from God because we are not doing His will. It also has workplace-specific consequences. Think for a moment about a coworker who has in some way hurt you and whom you have to date refused to forgive. In all likelihood, what this person said or did to you remains almost as fresh in your mind as the day it happened. You may remember even the smallest detail about the incident, whereas you remember nothing else about that particular day. Chances are that the resentfulness you originally felt still simmers. The residual anger from the incident has taken up indefinite residence in your heart. Unforgiveness perpetuates bitterness.

It also besets us with guilt. We know we should forgive, yet we reject this option. For whatever reason, we just cannot bring ourselves to clear this person's slate, and as we should, we feel bad about this. Refusing to forgive our coworkers sentences us Christians to cope with guilt each workday, thereby depriving us of full contentment with our work environments.

And not only does the quality of our work life suffer, but also our productivity may decline. It is burdensome and distracting to hold a grudge. We lose concentration at work. We actively try to avoid the person who hurt us. Many times because this is a person with whom we must work closely, we're less effective because of the invisible wall that separates us.

We can unilaterally dismantle that wall, if we so choose, through the radical alternative of forgiveness. We can, plainly and simply, say yes to God and no to our carnal, prideful stubbornness. Moreover, we can, through the following three steps, maintain a forgiving spirit throughout our work lives.

Maintaining a Forgiving Spirit

To do this, to make a forgiving spirit a permanent attribute, we must first undertake what is a formidable task for any human being: we must pray for those who persecute us. We should keep these persons and their needs in our daily prayers. Since *it is virtually impossible to remain angry at someone for whom we are praying*, we can remove a major obstacle to forgiveness through prayer.

Second, we should remain focused on the incredible magnitude of God's forgiveness. Chuck Swindoll has used a disturbing but powerful example of the incomprehensible depth of the Lord's grace to remind us of our reciprocal responsibility toward our neighbor. Suppose you have a six-year-old son, he begins, and suppose that one day you learn that your son is horribly murdered by a ruthless killer. If you do everything in your power to exact punishment on this killer, if you hunt him down and do to him what he did to your son, that's vengeance. If you leave to the civil authorities the task of locating the killer, trying him in a court of law, finding him guilty, and imposing a sentence for his crime, that's justice. But if you pardon this man, if you bring him to your house, and if you adopt him as your own son, that's grace.

No person I have ever known could engage in such a course of action. The enormity of God's grace seems to lie well beyond the outer boundaries of our own capacities. However, the illustration is invaluable not only because it offers us insight into God's limitless forgiveness but also because it puts the injustices that we endure at work in proper perspective. God forgives a debt we could never repay. He forgives even the most horrible sins and then warmly welcomes us prodigals back home. Against this backdrop, compare our unwillingness to forgive the relatively frivolous wrongs inflicted upon us by our coworkers. Our reluctance to forgive then seems embarrassing, and it exposes our ingratitude to God. We can overcome this ingratitude and develop a permanent forgiving spirit by always remaining mindful of how often and how unconditionally the Lord forgives us.

Third, and somewhat relatedly, we must permit Christ to rule our hearts. Hard-heartedness and self-direction inhibit our forgiveness, our joy, and our freedom from the bondage of this world for which Christ died. As will be discussed in chapter 8, relinquishing our lives to Christ transforms us from the inside out. And when this transformation happens, we will begin to see our persecutors not as enemies but as the Lord himself sees them—as our brothers and sisters, as compatriots struggling with the same pressures that we are, and as, in some cases, lost individuals who need to know Christ. Among the many blessings that come with affording Christ unrestricted control of our lives is a forgiving spirit. He eradicates the barriers to forgiveness and blesses us with a willingness to forgive our coworkers as many times as we are wronged.

And Once You Have Forgiven . . .

In closing this section, it is important to relate one word of caution: once you do forgive a coworker, it may be imprudent to tell him or her. Typically, it would be foolhardy to simply walk up and say something like, "By the way, I've completely forgiven you for ridiculing me in Tuesday's meeting and for that anti-Christian remark you made on Thursday." Such a statement will likely meet with indignation and possibly hostility. Often, a coworker who has hurt us does not think he or she needs to be forgiven for anything. On the contrary, from the opposite perspective, *you* may be the offender. "You're forgiving me?" the person might think. "How sanctimonious! You're the one who needs forgiveness, pal!" Ironically, your well-intentioned comment may drive rather than remove the wedge.

Instead of taking this risk, communicate your forgiveness by doing something nice for the person you forgive; make some sort of sacrifice. The work environment offers myriad opportunities to do this. Buy the person a cup of coffee, help him or her look for something he or she lost, fill in for the person if for some reason he or she must temporarily be away from work, take the time to ask about that coworker's family and be genuinely interested in the response, or say something complimentary about that person's work in the next meeting. *Show, don't tell about forgiveness.* You'll be amazed at how a simple act of kindness can drain the resentment.

Conclusion

Toward the end of what seemed to be the longest day of Mark's life, after almost everyone had gone home, Peter, a colleague who had been at lunch with Mark, stopped by his cubicle. Mark could not recall whether Peter contributed to the noontime onslaught, so he was not sure what to expect. Everything from lunch was still a bit blurry, and quite frankly, Mark did not care to remember it clearly anytime soon. Peter checked to make sure no one was in earshot and then remarked,

"That was one gutsy move at lunch, buddy. I've been here seven years, and I've never seen someone take a stand for their principles the way you did."

Mark nodded but did not smile. Right now, the last thing he wanted was conversation that would alienate him even further. But Peter had no such intention. Rather than questioning Mark's faith or advising Mark to back off of religion at work, Peter said: "I want you to know that you're not alone here. Wendy Jameson and I are both believers. So is Tanya over in actuarial and Steve DeVries in commercial sales. There are probably a lot more, too, but you can never tell because no one ever talks about it."

"That's good to know," Mark replied a bit stoically. "Thanks for telling me."

He wanted to ask Peter why he didn't come to his defense at lunch, but he thought better of it. Besides, the answer was implicit in Peter's hushed tone. What mattered right now was that Mark felt the weight of isolation lifted from him. Thoughts of meeting Peter's friends began to displace thoughts of revising his résumé.

"Gotta go," Peter said with a grin. "We'll talk soon."

The next day, Mark arrived early with enough bagels for the whole department.

———·———

Face it. You work in the lions' den. You operate within a culture that changes people, usually for the worse. Conflict, personal attacks, gossip, stress—they're everywhere. But so are needs. And so is God.

It is possible to radically alter our perspective toward our coworkers from one of adversity or indifference to one of servanthood and outreach. We can begin to view those around us as people under duress who require our forbearance, our compassion, and our assistance in carrying their burdens. We can adopt Christ's servant mind-set in all of our relationships, seeking to give more than we get.

On the job and elsewhere, we Christians also need to accept the inevitability of attacks on our faith. When we live and speak the truth, we cannot escape at least some derision. The Lord calls us, not to elude or confront such insults, but to the less-traveled roads of patience, endurance, and forgiveness. When a coworker attacks you for your convictions, control your emotions, smile politely, forgive him or her, and then bask in the assurance that the Lord blesses those who are persecuted for His sake.

In sum, when dealing with difficult people and thorny coworker issues on the job, trust the Lord's wisdom over the world's. In doing so, you will give glory to God and remove the shackles of tension and discontentment that so many of us live with at work. You will be liberated to love, serve, and work with those around you as Christ would.

3

Witness While You Work

MARK WAS BUSILY PECKING AWAY at his word processor when Curt, a sales manager, passed by his cubicle. Pointing to the Bible that Mark kept on his desk, Curt quipped, "Do you actually read that thing or is it just for show?"

"I read it every day," Mark replied with a smile. He had recently decided to keep the Book on his desk to invite inquiries just like these and prompt discussions of the gospel with his coworkers. "There's wonderful guidance and inspiration in here," he continued. "Do you have a copy?"

"I did a few years ago when I was in college," Curt responded with a smirk. "We used it to kill roaches in my apartment. We would say things like 'You have sinned against God, and I sentence you to death,' and then give them a good whack!"

Mark's heart sank as Curt laughed uncontrollably at his impressive wit. Mark assumed the conversation was over and returned his attention to the computer screen when he heard the question he was expecting from Curt in the first place. "Seriously, though," he said still beaming, "what do you see in all of this religion stuff anyway?"

Here was an opportunity for which he had prayed. Someone at work was asking why he was a Christian. This was a critical moment, and Mark knew that the next words out of his mouth could either perpetuate or obliterate whatever curiosity Curt had in Jesus. Without a quick, 30-second answer on the tip of his tongue, Mark astutely bought himself some time, responding, "Well, I can't answer that in a sound bite, but we can talk about it over lunch later. Are you free?"

———-———

Why Evangelize at Work?

The world is full of Curts. They're everywhere. Many know little or nothing about Christianity but are curious. Others were raised Christian and simply have strayed. Some have been wounded by religious experiences. Some have bought into the distortion of Christianity by the media and entertainment industry. Many have been deceived by the New Age movement, which attracts well-meaning, compassionate individuals by championing tolerance, religious pluralism, and value-neutral, standardless spirituality.

In almost all cases, these "seekers," as they are often called, are wandering spiritually because they have never had the gospel of Jesus Christ properly explained to them. Moreover, they have seldom seen it modeled by the behavior of those professing to be Christians. They therefore dismiss the potential of Christianity and search elsewhere in vain for answers to their eternal questions about the meaning of life, the proper way to live, and the afterlife. Their thirst for practical guidance on relationships, marriage, parenting, and career is never quenched as they rely on society's transient rules, quick fixes, and elixirs. Such reliance has culminated in countless broken lives.

And now before you stands a cynical but still curious Curt who may be giving you a brief window of opportunity to change his life.

But why should we evangelize at work or anywhere else for that matter? Evangelism is both difficult and time-consuming. Why expend tremendous effort and expose ourselves to public ridicule by sharing Christ with the Curts of our workplaces? Quite simply, because God asks us to.

The Great Commission in Matt. 28:19-20 instructs Christians to spread the good news of the gospel. It doesn't put limitations on where or when; it just says to do it. Furthermore, the Bible expounds on this, directing that in addition to modeling Christ for others through our lives and our actions, we must also *verbally* communicate our faith. Rom. 10:14, for example, candidly and powerfully makes this point: "How, then, can they call on the one they have not believed in? And how can they believe in the one of whom they have not heard? And how can they hear without someone preaching to them?" Similar instruction comes from Acts 8:31, where an Ethiopian seeker asks Philip how he can possibly understand the Book of Isaiah "unless someone explains it to me." And lest we think there is any loophole because we don't know Scripture well enough, 1 Pet.

3:15 punctuates our responsibility to articulate God's Word to others, stating, "Always be prepared to give an answer to everyone who asks you to give the reason for the hope that you have." That is, we need to understand our faith in enough depth to fully explain it when someone asks what we see in "this religion stuff."

It is reasonably clear, then, that our duty to witness goes well beyond keeping the Lord's commandments, being a "good person," and hoping that other people notice. Evangelism is a calling that compels all of us to also open our mouths—even in the workplace. But before we do, before we utter one word in the defense or explanation of our faith, it is *essential* that we first open our hearts and adopt an appropriate mind-set toward our coworkers.

Opening Our Hearts to Evangelism

Sharing the Word of God is the most awesome of responsibilities. Nothing compares to it. Not only is there the tremendous potential to change individuals' lives and the lives of their families, but also a person's salvation may hinge upon the very words you choose to impart. That's a pretty imposing task. Add to this the possibility that the person to whom you're speaking may be offended, and it's no wonder that the mere thought of witnessing terrifies many Christians. However, we can overcome our reluctance and reach our evangelistic potential for the Lord if we first open our hearts to a very important truth: *We have never looked into the eyes of someone who does not matter to God.*

No matter what people do for a living, no matter their religious background, no matter whether or not they attend church, and no matter how they act, they still matter to God. We all know this deep down, but it seems to be a difficult concept for many of us Christians to really accept. As we drive to church on Sundays, we see lots of people doing yardwork, running errands, playing sports, and doing a hundred other things instead of going to worship, and we fall into the trap of judging them for their irreverence. We watch the news and hear of all types of miscreants, and we think ourselves so much better. We see our coworkers stealing supplies, gossiping, or cheating on their spouses, and we somehow feel superior. As a natural consequence of this thinking, we become impatient and easily annoyed with people. Marinated in our self-righteousness, we stop caring about others. A personalized license plate I saw recently succinctly captured this attitude: UBUGME.

Many of us then make the fatal error of creating God in our own image: we assume that because we don't care about these people, God doesn't either. We conclude, although we never articulate this, that we've earned some sort of higher status with the Lord than has the nonbeliever or the nominal Christian. This is a pernicious line of reasoning because we are not only distorting the nature of God but also giving ourselves an airtight excuse not to spread His word. "After all," we subconsciously rationalize, "these are bad people, and since God does not want anything to do with them, why should I waste my precious time on them?"

In reality, we all matter equally to God. Regardless of our religion, our skin color, our ethnicity, or our sinfulness, God loves all of His children. And He wants us to follow His example. Jesus instructed us, without qualification or equivocation, to love our neighbor as ourselves. No value judgments. No strings attached. No sorting people into categories of those worthy and those unworthy of our love. He simply told us to love them all unconditionally. And as hard as I've tried, I've never found an exception for one's coworkers.

"Love my coworkers?" you might say. "*Love* them? I don't even *like* most of these people."

"Love them," says the Lord.

"But, Lord, You heard how Barbara insulted me the other day."

"Love them."

"And what about Margaret, Lord? She's been out to get me since day one."

"Love them."

"Even Frank, Lord? You can't mean Frank! He didn't even give me a raise last year, and he *never* gives me time off when I ask for it!"

"Love them."

"But . . ."

"But nothing. Love your neighbor as yourself."

End of discussion. God does not negotiate. Our job is simply to be faithful to that which He has commanded. To do so, we must adjust our mind-set to parallel God's mind-set. We must dispel this myth we've concocted about the existence of some supernatural pecking order. We need to see people in our workplace as God sees them.

In chapter 2, we considered techniques to develop the virtues of servanthood and a forgiving spirit. Here, in discussing the related but broader responsibility of love, it may be helpful to supplement those ideas with two more.

To begin this radical adjustment, jot down a few favorite Scripture verses on the principle of loving thy neighbor, and hang them someplace at work where you will see them many times each day. Two verses staring me squarely in the face when I sit down at my desk each day are 1 John 4:8 ("Whoever does not love does not know God, because God is love") and Phil. 2:3 ("Do nothing out of selfish ambition or vain conceit, but in humility consider others better than yourselves"). There are scores of other appropriate verses for this purpose.

Periodically, throughout the day, look at the verses you have chosen, and reflect on their wisdom. Think about them as you interact with people. Pray that no matter the circumstances, you will pursue their ideals. You will in time be blessed with a loving heart and a genuine concern for your coworkers' salvation.

It may also be beneficial to meditate each day on God's infinite love for you (posted verses might assist here as well). Once we gain even a glimpse of the magnitude of this love, once we begin to feel its extraordinary warmth and security, we cannot help but feel love for others. When we allow God to love us completely, our attitude toward everyone changes, including the Barbaras, Margarets, and Franks of the world. This loving attitude is the foundation on which we can pursue the Great Commission.

So to effectively witness at work, the starting point is to let the Lord drain whatever resentment or indifference you may feel toward your coworkers. Let Him show you that your ability to love other people has everything to do with what's inside of you and nothing to do with how these people act. Allow Him to fill your heart so that evangelism will become more privilege than obligation.

Overcoming Our Apprehension

Let's not kid ourselves, though. Even if we do learn to love our colleagues and even if we do come to view sharing the gospel as a privilege, the act of witnessing may still be a daunting task. "After all," many Christians say, "who am *I* to undertake such an awesome responsibility? How can *I* do justice to God's Word? And how can *I* possibly navigate all of the roadblocks to witnessing in a secular workplace?"

These are fair questions, but they reflect a mind-set that says, "I'm just a nobody who is powerless against the world, and since I'm powerless, there is no sense in even attempting to change anybody or anything." That's not scriptural. In fact, it is absolutely contrary to what the Bible says about what we can do when we invoke the power of the Holy Spirit that dwells within each one of us.

Dozens of verses attest to this, but among the most plain is 1 John 4:4, which tells us to remain cognizant that "the one who is in you is greater than the one who is in the world." Later in this book, John supplements this by assuring us that through Christ, we can overcome anything that the world throws at us (5:4-5). *Anything.* No exception is made for a coworker who is actively hostile to our worldview. We can overcome this. No caveat exists for our perception that we have insufficient theological knowledge to be an appropriate witness. We can overcome this. There is no qualifier that exempts us because we are wimpy or because we worry about what our coworkers will think of us. This, too, we can overcome.

There are two keys to gaining the requisite courage to be an effective witness. The first is *persistent prayer* as demonstrated by Eph. 6:19: we should pray that "whenever [we] open our mouth[s], words may be given so that [we] will fearlessly make known the mystery of the gospel." Thus, when we feel apprehensive about evangelism, we should pray for the love and compassion that will open our hearts to witnessing to our co-workers, pray for frequent workplace evangelism opportunities, pray that we will be able to deliver the message of the gospel concisely and convincingly, pray for the patience to endure the trials that will inevitably occur, and pray that the Lord will give us the fortitude and the wisdom to bring some of our coworkers to Christ. God will not let you down. "You may ask me for anything in my name," Jesus said in John 14:14, "and I will do it."

The second key to building courage is *practice*. Witnessing is a skill, like playing a sport or a musical instrument. And as with any skill, the more we practice it, the more adept and more confident we become. I am a better classroom instructor now than I was at the beginning of my career because of practice. Moreover, I am seldom anxious at the prospect of walking into a new class. Experience leads to both proficiency and confidence. Similarly, many who were at first fearful and shaky behind the wheel of a car have now mastered the skill of driving. They are no longer nervous on the road because of their considerable driving experience.

Witnessing is no different. Evangelism experience quells our fears and improves our abilities. We won't do it perfectly at first, but the second time will be better. And the third time will be better than that. As with any skill, confidence in witnessing is largely a function of practice.

What Does Not Seem to Work in Evangelism

Once we have established a foundation for evangelism by addressing issues of the heart, we can then begin to use our heads to distinguish between evangelism techniques that work and those that meet with very limited success. We'll start with the latter.

Using an Evangelism Style That Does Not Fit Your Personality

First things first: there is no "one right way" to spread God's Word. There's no exact blueprint in Scripture that must be followed to the letter by all witnesses. Rather, the Lord has designed each of us with certain talents and abilities that enable us to develop our own unique and effective evangelism style. He has equipped us with a brain to be innovative and imaginative in such situations.

Thus, the gregarious individual might use his or her ability to make close friends as a springboard to sharing God's truths. Such a person likely has the personality to also run a spirited and educational Bible study either before or after work or during lunch. The introverted individual, on the other hand, may find more suitable the strategy of candidly sharing the personal story of how God has changed his or her life. Alternatively, this shy person could simply invite people to church for worship and let the pastor's message stimulate a dialogue that would be awkward to begin otherwise. A husband and wife may find that they operate well as a team when socializing with other couples. A person who enjoys sports could disciple similarly minded colleagues through, for example, sports-related metaphors and illustrations. One who is skilled at debating might find the Socratic method to work best.

There are innumberable ways to evangelize and your effectiveness will in large part be determined by how well you apply the natural gifts God has given you. Before you say a word about Christ, then, take an inventory of these gifts and prayerfully consider how you may maximize your evangelism potential through them. Do not be deceived into believing that there is only one prototypical approach that you must use. This will almost certainly undermine your success as a witness.

Approaching Strangers

One quick way to be labeled a religious nut and to severely restrict opportunities to witness at work is to approach coworkers with whom you have not built any relationship. Most people consider religion to be an intensely personal matter. It is one of those things that defines an individual's self-concept. Not surprisingly, then, it is little wonder that people do not take kindly to strangers' solicitation of this private information. It seems like prying. It seems offensive and disrespectful. Such information is shared only in the strictest confidence with trusted friends.

This is why it is imperative to build a relationship with a person as a *prerequisite* to witnessing. This is not difficult in the workplace because our jobs are a social outlet where we develop some of our closest friendships. We interact with our coworkers for several hours each day. Some weeks we spend more time with these people than we do with our own families. This is fertile ground to lay the relational foundation for witnessing.

One resource that offers significant insight into finding strategic opportunities to witness through relationships is *Becoming a Contagious Christian* by Bill Hybels and Mark Mittelberg.[1] Here the authors argue that one effective evangelism technique that Jesus modeled for us is "rubbing shoulders with irreligious people." Jesus built bridges to nonbelievers by approaching them on their terms, by eating in their homes, and by meeting their needs as a friend would. He befriended all types of people, even those considered to be the dregs of society, and then proceeded to share the truth with them. He gained their trust and then revealed God's Word. We, accordingly, should emulate Him by investing time in our coworkers before sharing Christ. We should establish strong relationships at work and *only then*, if the Lord prompts us, use this foundation to spread the Good News.

Arguing the "Rightness" of Christianity

There's probably no faster way for a first conversation about Christ to degenerate into an argument than for a believer to claim or even imply that Christianity is "right" and that all other beliefs are "wrong." This is especially true in our postmodern culture where many have been deceived or browbeaten into accepting that *everything is relative* and that there is no such thing as absolute right and wrong. "Something may be right for you but it's not for me," they will reply indignantly, insulted by the perceived arrogance of the assertion. The purveyors of political correctness have duped this person, who, although willing to discuss matters of personal faith, is currently unwilling to accept the possibility that absolute truth and absolute right and wrong exist.

Rather than get philosophical or argumentative in such a situation, one useful alternative, as advanced in popular resources like *How Shall We Reach Them?*[2] (Michael Green and Alister McGrath), is to initially avoid the whole question of whose religion is right (a debate that is seldom productive) by instead testifying to the *attractiveness* of Christianity. That is, steer the conversation toward the joy that exists in your life because of Jesus. And as you do, be animated. Display your exuberance. Speak honestly from your heart, and don't worry whether you are making perfect sense or using all of the correct 10-dollar words. Your effervescence will attest to the genuineness of your beliefs and dynamically communicate that Christianity is appealing.

Furthermore, this approach will almost *never* culminate in

an argument. That's because it's almost impossible to argue with someone who is authentically testifying to what he or she feels inside. What can one say to the contrary? "No, you don't really feel that way"? The more likely result of this strategy is that any questions about right and wrong will become less significant as this person's thoughts turn to wondering whether he or she, too, might attain the uninhibited joy that you experience.

You can deliver poignant testimony while reserving "questions of truth" for later. By portraying Christianity as attractive, you implant the critical question that we hope all nonbelievers will contemplate: "Is there something to this Christianity stuff after all?"

Threatening Hell

Because fear can be a tremendously powerful motivator, many people attempt to exploit our fears to serve their own needs. We see this strategy employed in advertising as companies apprise us of how unsafe, boring, or otherwise meaningless our lives will be without their product. We see it in politics, especially in election years, as politicians forewarn us about the cataclysmic damage that the other party's agenda will inflict on society. We certainly see it in the workplace where some bosses seek to increase productivity by continually threatening their subordinates with termination.

People also make major life decisions based almost entirely on fear. Some marry the wrong person because they fear never finding someone else. Teenagers try drugs and alcohol because of the fear of not being "cool." College students sometimes select business or engineering majors not because they have any interest in the area but because they fear the possibility of not having a job immediately after graduation if they were to pursue a liberal arts degree. Fear clearly underlies many of the choices we make.

It is no wonder, then, that so many Christians attempt to predicate their witnessing on the abysmal consequences of not accepting Jesus as Lord. The tactic is expedient, penetrating, and leaves little room for debate. "What happens after you die?" they challenge. "You either live forever in paradise or you burn in hell. Your choice; take it or leave it." Or they say things like,

"Did you ever put your hand in a red-hot oven? Try it sometime, and then think about spending all of eternity in there!"

Anyone who has tried this approach knows, however, that such attempts to capitalize on one's fear of damnation seldom produce the desired result. If there is any impact at all, it is typically like that of a fad diet that may generate some temporary weight loss but almost always results in all of the weight coming back on. You may get some people thinking by threatening hell, but the stream of thought usually dissipates after a week or two, and ultimately, nothing changes in their lives. The weight they were carrying before remains.

In the scenario that opened this chapter, Mark could have responded to Curt by rambling, "I read the Bible and believe in the divinity of Jesus Christ, because if I don't, I will burn in a lake of sulfur for all of eternity, and you will, too, if you don't get down on your knees right now and repent, you sinner!" Had he done this, it's safe to predict that he would have won no points and maybe even affirmed Curt's suspicion that these Christians are raving lunatics who have no real answers to the questions that plague him.

And what a tragedy if this happens! Here is a seeker, perhaps someone who has an urgent need to hear the gospel of love and forgiveness, and instead of meeting the compassionate face of Christ through Mark, he is told that he has one more problem to worry about. "Who needs that?" many in his position will think. "And who wants to worship a God whose one dimension is fire and brimstone? I'm outta here."

A better approach, it seems, and one that is similar to dealing with the "rightness" of Christianity, is to defer the issue of eternal consequences until you have had a few constructive conversations about the attractiveness of Christianity. Seekers primarily want to know what *value* there is to believing, and although fear may lead them to reluctant decisions in some areas of their lives, it generally will not work here. They have a dire need, a hunger inside of them, a vacuum in their heart, something so pressing that it has stimulated them to broach the most delicate of topics with you. Tell them how Jesus has changed your life. Show them that Christianity is an inviting alternative to everything else that they've tried and has failed them. Do not squander this opportunity and chase them away by first pre-

senting God's standards, wrath, and judgment. If possible, focus on His love, forgiveness, and compassion, and deal with the
standards later.

"You Just Have to Have Faith"

In almost every substantial conversation of this type, the
question arises, "Why should I believe the Bible and not something else?" This is a very legitimate question that unfortunately stumps many Christians. We believe because we believe. We
have *faith* that the Bible is true. It's a core assumption that few
of us ever think about.

However, when we respond to a nonbeliever that "you just
have to have faith that this is true," what they often hear us say
instead is, "I have no real evidence for this, but take my word
for it anyway." Or worse, we may sound to them like the
proverbial used-car dealer who is trying to sell a lemon.

It's only natural for people to want some substantiation for
our claims. Why should they change their whole way of thinking, completely disrupt their lives, and surrender their old
selves, which in many cases do not seem so bad to them after
all, to adopt something for which there is no proof? "Have faith,
you say? Simply trust you on this one? Perhaps I should also
have faith that we should hole ourselves up in a Waco, Texas,
facility and await Armageddon!"

We must avoid sounding blind or cultic in responding to
this question because often our response determines whether
future conversations with this person will even exist. People
asking such a thing may want to believe in Christ but find their
intellect continually getting in the way. Others are relativists
who currently see all religions as equally valid or simply different paths up the same mountain. It is our job to demonstrate
that collectively these religions are like a maze where one path
leads to the ultimate objective. With many people we can only
do that by proffering evidence of biblical truth.

Many resources speak to this question, and you may want
to point your friend in these directions. However, doing things
such as tossing this person a copy of *Mere Christianity* and hoping that it will have an impact can only be effective if he or she
actually reads and studies it. Often a person will not, so you
will need to cogently make the case yourself.

The specifics of such an argument can be found in volumes such as *Evidence That Demands a Verdict*[3] by Josh McDowell and *The New Testament Documents: Are They Reliable?*[4] by F. F. Bruce, and from organizations such as the Christian Research Institute and Christian Answers.[5] Here are but a few examples of the incisive apologetic points they advance:

- The Bible contains nearly 2,000 prophecies concerning almost every nation within a thousand miles of Jerusalem. Archaeological confirmations of these prophecies have been almost innumerable over the last century. In fact, Dr. Nelson Glueck, considered among the foremost scholars on Israeli archaeology, is quoted as saying, "No archeological discovery has ever controverted a Biblical reference. Scores of archeological findings have been made which confirm in clear outline or in exact detail historical statements in the Bible. And, by the same token, proper evaluation of Biblical descriptions has often led to amazing discoveries."[6] Doesn't such unblemished accuracy legitimize the Bible as a trustworthy account of historical events?

- The Old Testament also contains more than 300 *specific* prophecies concerning the birth, life, death, and resurrection of the Messiah (e.g., that He would be born in Bethlehem [Mic. 5:2], that He would be born of a virgin [Isa. 7:14], that His hands and feet would be pierced [Ps. 22:16], and that He would be crucified with transgressors [Isa. 53:9, 12]). These prophecies are not vague generalities, as we see in so many other religions and from people such as Jeanne Dixon and Nostradamus, but are precise and verifiable. Most importantly, they were all fulfilled by the life of Jesus Christ. In light of the historical accuracy of the Old Testament, these fulfilled prophecies are compelling evidence for the divinity of Christ.

- The writers of the Bible claimed repeatedly that they were delivering the infallible and authoritative Word of God. These 40 or so men were either telling the truth or they were lying fanatics. Is it really plausible that a group of wackos could have collectively produced the most perfect moral code in human history? And is it reasonable to believe that madmen could generate a collection of 66 books over 1,600 years that is so internally consistent? The only logical explanation is divine inspiration.

In sum, then, asking people to accept the Bible on faith often precludes further dialogue. It's a conversation killer. Conversely, a more cerebral response to this question that introduces the nonbeliever to the overwhelming evidence for biblical truth can be the gateway to a continued exchange of ideas. And often it also becomes the basis for genuine belief.

Some Practical Advice for Witnessing at Work

There are a multitude of resources that focus entirely on evangelistic techniques. Many of these are available through commercial publishing houses, several can be obtained through radio ministries, and an ever-increasing number can be downloaded from the Internet for little or no cost. What follows here, some practical advice on evangelizing in the workplace, is but a tiny subset of the wealth of available guidance.

Before You Ever Say a Word About Christ

- First, get your own spiritual house in order. No one is going to take you seriously if you seem hypocritical and do not walk your lofty talk. Live a sanctified lifestyle, and model Christ for your coworkers in everything you do.

- Make a list of coworkers who you think have a special need to hear the Word of God. Keep this list to between three and eight people so that you may pray daily and effectively for opportunities to teach them. Pray as Col. 4:3 instructs, "that God may open a door for our message, so that we may proclaim the mystery of Christ."

- As noted earlier, build friendships with those you seek to reach before you witness to them. Go to lunch with these people, stay late to assist them with their work, and if possible, socialize with them after work. Lay the groundwork for successful evangelism by demonstrating your (and God's) love for them.

- Place things on your desk or in your work area that invite inquiry about your religious beliefs. Leave a Bible in plain sight. Make available a small basket of Christian literature. Use a Bible verse calendar and, if you have a computer, a Bible verse screen saver. In doing so, you can identify the seekers in your workplace. Bumper stickers, T-shirts, and even quotations on business cards are a few other nonthreatening vehicles for stimulating conversation. Workplace evangelism is more efficient if you can get seekers to come to you.

- It is essential that we have knowledge of God's Word before we proclaim it. That is, we should not begin to teach until we are able to teach. This entails studying Scripture and thinking through answers to common questions such as, "What is Christianity?" "Why are you a believer?" and "How do you know the Bible is true?" Resources such as a topical analysis of the Bible, a Bible dictionary, and a concordance will be valuable here. Also, the Internet has a plethora of free materials to educate us, including evangelism and apologetics web sites and online study libraries.

- Turn conversations from the mundane to the meaningful. The most effective witnesses are those who have mastered the art of casually steering a conversation toward issues of God and faith. On the job, we continually talk with our coworkers about some of the most superficial (and safe) topics. The weather, the day's headlines, Jay Leno's monologue, our bosses' idiosyncracies, and so forth. On rare occasions, and with only one or two trusted coworkers, we broach the more personal issues of what's really going on in our lives and how we are feeling about it. These social norms can make workplace evangelism difficult. Thus, we need to overcome them and find a way to move discussions from the superficial to the spiritual.

  There are several ways to do this, many of which involve subtly incorporating religious inquiries and comments into the conversation. For instance, if a new coworker has just moved into town, you could ask if he or she has found a good church. In doing so, you've just communicated that religion is important to you and that such issues are not beyond your boundaries of discussable topics. You'll also get information here that may tell you about this person's spiritual needs and whether there is fertile ground for witnessing. Other discreet avenues include such things as inquiring about the religious jewelry someone is wearing, bringing up what you did over the weekend at your church, and mentioning something you heard on a Christian radio broadcast.

We need to take some risks in conversation to open the door to what is all too often considered a taboo subject in the workplace. To do so, a good rule of thumb is to always look for openings in conversation where you can interject a religious-oriented comment, talk about your church, or diplomatically inquire about someone's beliefs.

- Keep in mind that you will not be able to reach everyone at work. Where time is very limited, it may be a good idea to give priority to those who currently have no religious affiliation whatsoever. These people, especially those claiming to be agnostic, tend to be a bit more receptive to faith discussions than are those in established denominations.

While You Are Witnessing

- To be understood, first seek to understand. This is a principle that applies not just in evangelism but in communication generally. The basic theory here is that if you listen carefully, if you restate the other person's points so that he or she knows you have understood, and if you sincerely attempt to comprehend what he or she is trying to say, you increase the likelihood that the person will in turn actively listen to what you have to say. In negotiations, it is often said that the cheapest concession one can make is to let the other side know that it's been heard. To maximize the impact of your message, make this "concession" each time a potential seeker speaks.

- Use the strategy of telling your personal story whenever you can. This is a powerful mechanism for spreading the Good News because you are offering irrefutable evidence that this is life-changing stuff.

- Be gentle in disagreement. When discussing sensitive issues such as religion, we will inevitably find ourselves disagreeing over some issues. Once this happens, we must be sure that the conversation does not become an argument. The Bible speaks specifically to this point, advising that "the Lord's servant must not quarrel; instead, he must be kind to everyone, able to teach, not resentful. Those who oppose him he must gently instruct, in the hope that God will grant them repentance leading them to a knowledge of the truth" (2 Tim. 2:24-25). Similar wisdom comes from Solomon, who wrote, "A gentle answer turns away wrath, but a harsh word stirs up anger" (Prov. 15:1).

Gentleness and kindness need be our hallmarks if we are to competently witness. When disagreement occurs, diffuse the situation by admitting in humility that you need to think about their point and then return to the discussion another day.

- Turn tough questions into opportunities. If you're like most people, you don't provide a particularly good response when you don't really know the answer to a question. When we try to bluff our way through the difficult questions that always seem to arise in conversations about Christianity, we sell the gospel short. We stumble through our answers and they become incoherent. We are not confident about what we're saying, and it shows.

Rather than attempting to provide an answer you do not immediately have, use this person's tough question as an opportunity to set up another conversation with him or her. Tell your friend that this is a great question and that to furnish a fully accurate answer, you need to look something up. Set up another time to discuss this point, and then, in the interim, do your homework and think through your response. In this way, tough questions can be a stepping-stone to further progress rather than a stumbling block.

After a Few Conversations

- Buy them a resource. There are lots of materials out there that can communicate the message of the gospel better than we can. Unfortunately, most nonbelievers will not make such purchases for themselves. If you have the financial means, buy some resource for them to supplement your witnessing.

Because people in our culture are always looking for a quick reference to resolve their problems, one of my favorite gifts is a topical analysis of the Bible. This resource demonstrates to the reader that the Bible addresses every life issue, and it enables the reader to efficiently gain scriptural instruction on whatever questions he or she has. Audiocassettes, videos, and booklets that explain the basics of Christianity also serve this purpose well.

- Invite them to your church. After your initial conversations about faith with a nonbeliever, it may be beneficial to expose him or her to someone else's perspective on the subject, namely that of a pastor or priest. The least threatening way to facilitate this is to invite your friend to a Sunday service or mass. If your friend agrees to go with you, determine when the most insightful speaker at the church will be delivering the message that week, and attend at that time. Afterward, take your friend out for coffee or brunch so that you may answer any questions he or she may have.

- Be cautious when witnessing to the opposite sex. Invariably, successful witnessing elevates the relationship of the people involved to the strongest type of friendship. Sharing someone's deepest concerns, attending church with someone, and praying with someone are all actions that promote affection and intimacy. Thus, if one is witnessing to a member of the opposite sex, one must remain cognizant of the potential for the relationship to extend beyond friendship. Depending on the marital status of the people involved, it may therefore be prudent for a witness, after making some progress with the seeker, to relinquish the role to someone of the seeker's same gender. In doing so, the witness minimizes temptations that can destroy marriages.

And in Closing . . .

- Invite them to accept Christ as their Lord and Savior. This is the whole purpose of these conversations, so at some point, and it may take years, we must extend this invitation. There is no "one right time" or "one right way" to do this, and in fact, there is much conflicting advice on appropriate approaches to what many consider an awkward and relationship-threatening moment. It seems that the best prescription comes, not surprisingly, from Scripture itself: "Do not be anxious about anything, but in everything, by prayer and petition, with thanksgiving, present your requests to God" (Phil. 4:6). We should pray for an appropriate moment and pray that the Lord will afford us the words and the wisdom to bring our friends to Christ.

Conclusion

Mark and Curt carried their trays to a remote area of the cafeteria where they engaged in the obligatory small talk that often precedes earnest discussions. After a brief lull in the conversation, Mark, in an enthusiastic but controlled voice, said, "Can I tell you a story about something that changed my life?"

————·————

Our jobs serve many pragmatic purposes, but they also provide us with an important opportunity to model Christ and to spread the gospel. The Lord implores us to accept and relish the responsibility to minister to coworkers who do not know Christ. He also reminds us that in doing so, we should be courageous but considerate, honest but humble, genuine but gentle, and persistent but patient. He calls us to live outside the comfort zone on the job and to do His work while we do our own.

4

How Hard Should Christians Work?

APPROXIMATELY 24 MONTHS into his job, Mark had become quite proficient at analyzing financial statements and performing all of the client service duties assigned to him. He was regarded as one of the most diligent employees in the department, was earning enough money to easily pay his bills, and was now being groomed for a managerial slot. Things had fallen in place nicely. Still, something important seemed to be missing from his work life—namely, purpose.

Before him on the desk sat yet another balance sheet from yet another new client. Mark rubbed his eyes and looked at his watch. 3:32. He glanced at the statement. "Accounts Receivable: $25,000; Inventory: $68,000 . . ." He took a sip of coffee and checked his E-mail. Nothing. He peeked his head out of the cubicle to see if there was someone—anyone—to divert his attention from the endless parade of debits and credits. No one there. He looked at his watch again. 3:34.

"What an empty existence," Mark thought. "Crunching numbers day in, day out. Answering to clients, jumping through their hoops. Spending 50 or 60 hours a week simply to help maximize profit for this faceless company I work for. There's got to be something more to work than earning a paycheck, moving up the ladder, and then retiring." 3:35.

———·———

There is. And the good news is you won't need to change jobs to find it.

Many of us see our work as mundane and our jobs as nothing more than a means to an economic end. We too seldom find personal fulfillment in work, even when we perform our jobs well. We anxiously await Fridays and dread Monday mornings. Our bosses are too critical, and our families do not appreciate how hard we work for them. To enhance the quality of our work lives and to bring us some sense of accomplishment, we often look toward raises and promotions only to later learn that the satisfaction we receive is short lived. Then, work returns to a rather routine and meaningless state.

That's a pretty dismal portrayal, and I wish I could say that it is an overstatement. But for millions of people in the U.S. workforce, it is an all-too-accurate representation of their daily lives. In fact, in 1995, citing a large employee satisfaction survey, *American Demographics* magazine reported, consistent with the results of many similar surveys, that more than 1 of every 3 U.S. workers is not satisfied with his or her work.[1] In a workforce of 100 million, that translates into about *35 million* dissatisfied employees!

But there's something even more troublesome about this statistic. Because our sense of personal worth is largely derived from the belief that we're accomplishing something important in our lives, perceiving our work as dissatisfying, menial, or purposeless may cause us to feel insignificant, not just as workers but as people. We often, like Mark, experience some personal void as a result. We perceive that we are missing something critical in our lives.

And in fact, we are. This sense of emptiness is far removed from what the Lord intends for us. As detailed in this chapter, God created work—all work—to be primarily a spiritual activity, not an economic or social activity. But as is so often the case, humankind's worldview does not comport with God's intent, and we thereby forfeit the valuable gift of purposeful work that He wants to provide. Consider for a moment just how different our secular perspective is from the Lord's instruction on the subject.

How the World Views Work

Two questions: why do we work, and how hard should we work? Ask these questions to anyone on the street (or any college student in a classroom, as I often do), and you'll see more than your fair share of frowns that say, "Those are sorta dumb questions, aren't they?" Everyone knows why we work. It's a necessary evil to put food on the table and to keep a roof over our heads. We toil to earn money so we can buy necessities and the occasional luxury. Sometimes the goal is a large bank account; sometimes it's subsistence. On a brighter note, though, some people, albeit a minority I think, will respond that they also work because it's gratifying and because they enjoy it.

On the question of effort, the answers are equally predictable. We work hard enough to remain employed, to keep the boss off our backs, to get raises, to move up if that is our ambition, or to make a comfortable level of income. To almost everyone the answers to these two questions are patently obvious.

Obvious, perhaps, but also insufficient. When we perceive work as a survival mechanism, as a vehicle to acquire things, or even as something pleasant to pass our time, we have misconstrued its intended purpose in our lives. When we expend only enough energy to get by, we are misunderstanding the Lord's plan for our work. Each day most of us operate under this set of worldly assumptions about work, overlook the possibility that God has some will for our employment, and, as a result, experience intermittent if not perpetual discontentment with our jobs. This utilitarian, secular perspective on work stands in sharp contrast with how God wants us to view our work.

How God Wants Us to View Work

If you had all the money that you'd ever need and you had plenty of interesting hobbies to occupy your time, would you still work? Would you regularly engage in some type of labor, whether paid or unpaid? I believe that for most people, the answer to this question is yes. My suspicion is that most people in this situation, both Christian and non-Christian alike, would pursue some type of daily or periodic activity to serve what they believe to be the common good. They might work with handicapped children or the elderly, or take up the banner of some other altruistic cause. They might work full-time as a homemaker and home-school their kids. They might pursue further education, work to develop their minds, and then use this education to make some contribution to society. People will work, even when no economic necessity exists.

And why is that? It's simply because work gives expression to our creative gifts and helps us to fulfill a responsibility we feel to improve the lives of our fellow citizens and of future generations. It offers us some way to satisfy a very basic need for meaning in our lives. If you're skeptical about this, examine it from the flip side: consider what happens to those who do not have any work. Anyone who's ever been jobless for some period of time can poignantly testify to unemployment's demoralizing and even dehumanizing effects. They know firsthand that work is intrinsic to the human condition and essential to sustain human dignity.

This is, of course, no accident. The Bible from its very first chapter illustrates that our innate desire to work is by God's design. Genesis opens with God working, creating the heavens and the earth, the day and the night, the water and the land, the sky, the birds, and all of the animals. He then creates humankind in His own image, calling people to imitate God in everything that they do, including work.

However, not only does the Lord communicate through His example that work is an inherent component of human existence, but also He commands it explicitly, instructing Adam and Eve (and us) to "be fruitful and increase in number; fill the earth *and subdue it*" (Gen. 1:28, emphasis added). To "subdue" the earth is to cultivate it, to transform it, and to adapt its resources. It is a task that clearly implicates labor. Even more plain is Gen. 2:15, which says, "The LORD God took the man and put him in the Garden of Eden to work it and take care of it." God has therefore created us to work, taught us by example to work, and specifically directed us to work.

But to what end? What exactly does the Lord want us to accomplish through our work? Did He simply invent work so that we could earn a living and thereby survive? Not at all. If survival were His concern, He could, as we do for our own children, simply provide food and shelter without requiring any labor. The Lord, therefore, must have created work for another purpose.

As noted in the introductory chapter of this book, the New Testament fully reveals this purpose. It tells us in several places exactly what our primary motivation for working should be. Col. 3:23-24 says it most directly:

> Whatever you do, work at it with all of your heart, as working for the Lord, not for men, since you know that you will receive an inheritance from the Lord as a reward. It is the Lord Christ you are serving.

This simple, illuminating passage tells us to perceive whatever we do—*everything we do*—as service to the Lord. In other words, when we go to school to become educated, it is to serve the Lord. When we raise a family, it is to serve the Lord. When we exercise, it is to serve the Lord. Even when we do something as seemingly frivolous as yardwork, it is for Him. And most pertinent here, when we pursue His command to "subdue the earth"—when we go to work each day—we are to consider our workplace tasks first and foremost as service to our Father. He's our Supreme Boss, our Divine Manager. It is to Him that we ultimately report. It is He who created our work, not as a curse and not as just a means to a paycheck, but to allow us to glorify Him through it. *This is the true meaning of work.* Moreover, in emulating God by working, we become more like Him and thereby gain dignity, self-worth, and fulfillment as a human being. Herein lies the reason that we all feel a need to work and to contribute to society, regardless of our financial situation.

Note also that none of this depends on what type of job you have. Whether you are digging ditches for a construction company or digging ditches as a missionary in China, your work gives glory to God. Homemaker, home builder, or home-run hitter, you are to serve the Lord in every facet of your work. An often-related story is that of Johann Sebastian Bach, the great composer, who inscribed S.D.G. on all of his compositions, standing for *Sola Deo Gloria*, "to the glory of God alone." Bach was an independent contractor who perceived himself as completely dependent. He could have been his own boss, but like Rembrandt, Michelangelo, and countless others of their time, he accepted direction and inspiration from a wiser Boss. Now, hundreds of years later and thousands of years after the Garden of Eden, God's purpose for work remains the same. He calls each of us to view work through His lens, not the world's, and to give Him glory through everything we do in the workplace.

In this light, the question about how hard we should work practically answers itself. If you really consider God to be your Boss, will you ever be late for work? Will you ever slack off and take the in-house vacation? Will you ever complain about an assignment or that your work is meaningless? And will you ever perform below your potential and call it good enough?

Of course not. Conceptualizing work in this way results in a transformation of one's attitude and a consequent elevation of personal productivity. If you're assembling televisions in a factory, for example, you're not simply building them for Zenith anymore, you're building them to please God. You're now responding to the Lord's incentives and performing your tasks according to His specifications. He's your quality control manager, and you know that He doesn't miss a thing. Laziness, a sin so grave that it is addressed in 14 separate chapters of Proverbs, will almost never be an issue because you will have shed the world's unmotivating vision of why you are working. As a result, maximum effort will come very naturally and you will, in fact, become the most industrious employee in the company, regardless of your pay and working conditions. Your drive for excellence will no longer vary with workplace circumstances but will remain as constant as your Father's instruction. In every responsibility you have in the workplace as a committed Christian, you will be a committed employee.

Once upon a Time, This Was the Norm

If such an approach to your work seems utopian or unattainable, consider this: until about the year 1900, most of the U.S. labor force indeed viewed work as God does. The Lord's perspective on work was inculcated at home, in elementary and secondary school (both public and private), and in almost all universities. Pastors regularly preached it from every pulpit in America, and it was passed on unblemished from generation to generation. It was what has been historically referred to as the Protestant work ethic.

Dating back to Martin Luther's contention that it is a Christian's duty to accept involvement in worldly affairs as a calling, Christians of many denominations have championed the virtues of diligence, austerity, reliability, thrift, and other such attributes in business affairs. For instance, the Puritan perspective, probably best articulated by Cotton Mather, was that it is good for men to rise in business and to serve God by making money. In more recent times, devout Christian business leaders such as John D. Rockefeller Jr. and James C. Penney earned their fortunes by viewing themselves as trustees of God's money and operating by biblical principles in everyday business affairs. In doing so, they disproved the notion that one could not be a committed Christian and a successful businessperson simultaneously.

And we can disprove that, too, every working day. We can choose God's view of work, honor Him through our jobs, and reap both eternal and temporal rewards as a result.

But beware. When you pursue a Christian level of productivity, your peers at work will inevitably notice and may try to resell you the world's competing perspective. As explained in chapter 2, a corporate culture exists in every workplace that often distracts us from Christlike behavior.

"You're being naive," your coworkers may tell you as you explain the divine underpinnings of your strong work ethic. "Hard work may still be a virtue these days, but you can't trust management here to reward you for it. Instead, this company will squeeze every last ounce of energy out of you and then not think twice about laying you off. Work harder and they'll simply ratchet up the standard. So if you're not getting paid for it or if your job's not on the line, don't waste your time doing extra stuff for them. You've gotta look out for No. 1 because management sure isn't going to look out for you."

And so the argument goes. The diatribe accelerates and spirals, leading to their impassioned and sometimes compelling bottom line, *you shouldn't work any harder than you have to.*

But don't be deceived. Those who advance such arguments, and you'll likely find several of them where you work, are completely missing the point. We work hard to glorify God. How we're rewarded on earth doesn't matter. Whether our company exploits that effort doesn't matter. We trust God, even if we do not trust our earthly boss.

Our work ethic is solely determined by God's blueprint. And if we can maintain this mind-set and this Christian level of productivity, not only do we remain in God's will, but also He blesses our work lives with job satisfaction, higher performance, and ultimately greater success in our careers. The only remaining question, then, is how to sustain this perspective daily so that we may continually receive these blessings.

Maintaining Your Productivity and Job Satisfaction Daily

There are plenty of books out there that advise managers how to cultivate a satisfied workforce, how to build employee morale, and how to motivate employees to maximize their potential. And some of this stuff actually works. But things like pay-for-performance, flexible work schedules, job rotation, employee empowerment, and all the rest of the trendy systems advanced to help firms gain a competitive advantage pale in comparison to the Lord's instruction on maintaining productivity and satisfaction. Here are two time-honored, scripturally based tips that always work when a Christian fully adopts them into his or her heart.

Remind Yourself Each Day That You Work for the Lord

Knowing the information presented above and living it each day are two separate things. We can say that we work first and foremost for God, and we can robotically acknowledge that He is our ultimate CEO, but without action, those are just empty words. And even if we are genuine in our desire to apply them, the pressures of the workplace, the corporate culture, and our entrenched habits on the job serve to undermine the long-term adoption of this mind-set. That is, we can initially be on fire to complete every task at work for His glory, but we may find that fire extinguished the next time we receive a boring assignment or are faced with arduous work. We therefore need a spark to reignite that fire each workday.

You may find it worthwhile to privately rewrite your job description to reflect that everything you do on the job is for God. Include in the description all of the tasks you normally would be required to perform, and then add something like, "Each of these tasks, without exception, is to be completed for the Lord, not for the company." Supplement this by placing both Col. 3:23 (quoted above) and Gal. 1:10 ("Am I now trying to win the approval of men, or of God? . . . If I were still trying to please men, I would not be a servant of Christ") in plain sight in your workstation, cubicle, or office. Whenever you are feeling lazy, bored, aggravated, or overwhelmed, read the new job description, reflect on the two verses, and allow the truth to rejuvenate your heart. Then say yes to the Lord and proceed with your work.

Choose the Right Attitude at Work

How many times have you heard someone say, "He needs an attitude adjustment"? Probably too many. You may have even heard, at some point, some such comment directed at you.

The phrase "attitude adjustment" has become commonplace in the American lexicon, perhaps as a result of individuals increasingly sporting bad attitudes. But it implies something that few people seem to realize. If one can adjust his or her attitude, then attitude is not something that is beyond our control. Rather, it is something we can regulate and something we tell people, in many cases, they should regulate. That is, *our attitude is simply a choice.*

Is this a revelation? For many it is. Most people seem to think that one's attitude is purely a function of what happens to a person. We are "victims of circumstance," accepting that what happens to us should dictate what happens in us. For example, we feel justified in having a dismal attitude if we are caught in an unhappy marriage, if we cannot find a job, or if we are feeling ill. We have no difficulty rationalizing our overt and extended frustration when we unexpectedly get stuck in traffic, miss an important appointment, and then get a 50-dollar speeding ticket on the way home. Our day is completely ruined, and everyone had best stay out of our way. In the workplace, too, our attitude can turn sour daily because of stressful or boring tasks, a demanding boss, too little pay, long hours, or because we feel that we work with a bunch of jerks. In such an exacting world, who wouldn't have a bad attitude? Who wouldn't, at some point at least, be in need of an attitude adjustment?

Jesus wouldn't. Jesus experienced problems far beyond those that will ever afflict most of us. People doubted Him, slandered Him, mocked Him, persecuted Him, and ultimately sentenced Him to an excruciatingly painful execution. Throughout, though, His attitude before people remained constant, encouraging, and exemplary.

The apostle Paul tells us in Phil. 2:5 that we are to act the same way, writing, "Your attitude should be the same as that of Christ Jesus." Our attitude is to be that of a humble servant: content no matter the circumstances, selfless, joyful, obedient to the Father, and willing to "do everything without complaining or arguing" (Phil. 2:14). We are to adopt—*to choose*—the attitude we see in Jesus. It's entirely up to each one of us, Paul says. We decide what our attitude will be.

So it is not the case, as the world would have us believe, that our attitude and our mood just happen to us. We're not born pessimistic, optimistic, or moody. We are not powerless to do something—something permanent—about our attitude.

Quite the opposite: we choose, consciously or not, to be exactly how we are.

Applying this principle to the work environment, it is apparent that no matter what type of job you have and no matter what the circumstances in your workplace, you can be content and highly productive. It does not matter that the work is monotonous or dirty or seemingly pointless. It does not matter that you may have to continually deal with irate or rude customers and coworkers. The quality of your work life can be regulated wholly by your personal perspective on the work. If you choose to view your job as service to God and simply decide to be satisfied with all you do, your work life will be fulfilling no matter what you are doing.

To assist you in this endeavor, consider taking to heart what have been life-changing verses for many throughout history:

> I have learned to be content whatever the circumstances. I know what it is to be in need, and I know what it is to have plenty. I have learned the secret of being content in any and every situation, whether well fed or hungry, whether living in plenty or in want. I can do everything through him who gives me strength *(Phil. 4:11-13)*.

Through the strength of the Lord, then, you can make an earnest decision this very minute to be happy with your job, with your work environment, and with those people around you. One of the greatest gifts that God has given us is the freedom and the ability to make choices about our lives. And He invites each of us to better our earthly lives by choosing the attitude of Christ.

Conclusion

To truly find purpose, satisfaction, and success in your job, start by dispensing with all of the preconceptions about work that society has fed you. They're wrong. Work is much more than a means to a paycheck and something to occupy our time. It is a directive, an invitation, and a gift from God. When we neglect to view it this way and instead buy into the world's pragmatic perspective of work, we often experience discontentment, strife, undue stress, and the empty feeling that our work is meaningless.

Your work life does not have to be this way. You have the keys to remove your own shackles. Step 1 is to consider today a completely different paradigm: you work for the Lord in everything you do. Every task you complete, every product you manufacture, every customer you serve, every call you take, every document you type—*everything you do*—should be conceptualized primarily as service to Christ.

Step 2 is to choose an attitude of contentment on the job regardless of circumstances. Although there will be those times that it makes sense (or you feel called) to change jobs, while working in any particular job, adopt the attitude that Christ would have. This will do more to affect the quality of your work life than will any amount of pay or any title you could earn. It will permit you to perpetually find satisfaction in your work no matter what the job entails.

Meaningful work, a strong work ethic, high productivity, job satisfaction, and, most importantly, faithfulness to the Lord's teaching on work can all be yours by remaining focused on the One who offers the ultimate paycheck.

5

A Right Response to Wrongful Treatment

*M*ARK'S BOSS CALLED HIM *into the office and invited him to sit down. It was time for his third annual review, and after all of the overtime he had put in the past 12 months, Mark was looking forward to a glowing evaluation, to the promise of a promotion, and to a substantial merit raise. He had already contemplated how he could upgrade his computer and stereo system with the extra income. He'd also envisioned how impressive his business cards would look with a new title imprinted under his name. Life was looking good as Mark's boss closed the door.*

And then it was looking not so good.

"I know you've been working hard," the silver-haired gentleman began, "so you're probably not going to be too happy with what I have to say." The boss then proceeded to rattle off a litany of improvements he wanted to see in Mark's performance over the next year—everything from fewer mathematical errors to clearer reports to working through more lunches. There would be no merit raise until he could show improvement in all areas.

Mark left the office both confused and bitter. He knew that what had transpired in the last 30 minutes just wasn't right. And to make his day complete, he learned later that afternoon that his friend David, who had been with the firm for only two years, received the promotion Mark was expecting.

———·———

Mark has a grievance, perhaps a legitimate one. It's simply not fair to give your best to an organization—to work evenings and weekends, to sacrifice family and social life, to endure a daily commute, and to return home with a headache—only to have that effort go unrecognized.

We've all been there in one way or another. Most of us know firsthand that the most infuriating facet of any job is the feeling that we're disrespected, unappreciated, discriminated against, underpaid, or otherwise treated inequitably. And when it happens, many of us have a tough time containing our anger. In all likelihood, as soon as Mark left his boss's office, his face communicated to everyone around him that now was no time to ask for a favor. He's at least annoyed and maybe closer to incensed. And who wouldn't be? No promotion *and* no raise after all that work? Mark may have been fortunate to escape from the office without firing off a few choice words not found in *Webster's*.

Anger is an inescapable part of the human condition. It is a powerful and complex emotion that consumes many who are treated subjectively or unjustly at work, often leading us to respond in ways that are displeasing to the Lord. To deal with these inevitable injustices in a manner that is scripturally sound, therefore, we should start by familiarizing ourselves with some of the dynamics of anger, specifically, why we get angry and what alternatives we have for releasing it. Then, using this foundation, we'll look at what the Bible teaches about properly expressing our anger after we've been treated unfairly.

Why We Get Angry and What We Typically Do About It

Two of the leading authorities in the area of anger management are Dr. Les Carter and Dr. Frank Minirth of the Dallas-based Minirth-Meier Clinic, one of the largest psychiatric clinics in the world. Their landmark work, *The Anger Workbook*,[1] serves as an ideal framework for understanding our anger and our options for responding to injustices perpetrated by our boss.

Boiled down to its essentials, the process by which we become angry and release that anger is depicted in Figure 5-1. Reading from left to right, our boss's behaviors, decisions, and feedback can make us angry for any or all of three reasons. First, we may feel disrespected or degraded by the boss. If, as with Mark, your boss rates your performance as below average or unacceptable when you've been putting forth extra effort for him all year long, you are likely to be angry because your *personal worth* is being devalued.

Furthermore, let's say that you get no raise because of this

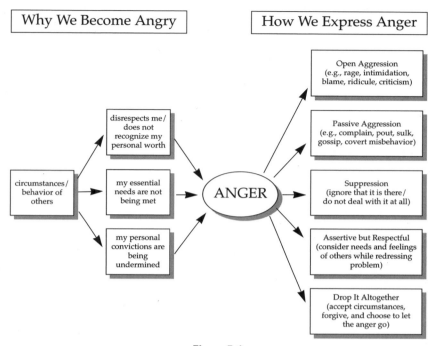

Figure 5-1

erroneous review. You were counting on the extra pay simply to keep up with inflation and to continue paying the bills. Now, in light of this evaluation, those payments will be tougher to make. You have some *essential needs*, in this case economic ones, that will go unmet because of your boss's appraisal. And often, that's an outrage to us. When a boss's actions cause essential needs to go unmet, such as the need for time with the family ("You *must* work this weekend"; "No, you cannot go home early to meet with your kid's teacher"), the need for sleep ("I want to see you here by 7:00 sharp every morning"), or the need for interesting work ("Sorry, we cannot redesign your job or let you rotate tasks. Company policy"), anger is a natural outcome.

Third, consider a situation where you do an exemplary job because, as discussed in chapter 4, you work in recognition of Christ as your CEO. Your work ethic is outstanding, and you take great pride in the product or service you produce. Your boss, however, advises you that while your work is good, you take too long to do it. He doesn't need perfection, just efficient performance.

This irritates you. "I work for God before I work for you," you might mumble under your breath. "And He *does* want perfection in my work." You are angry, but not because you feel disrespected; he complimented your work. Nor are you angry because some personal need is left wanting by the boss's comment. Rather, your anger here is probably a function of your values being demeaned. Anger is generated by the undermining of our *personal convictions.* For this reason, we get angry when a politician votes the "wrong" way, when a judge or jury renders a ridiculous verdict, or when the media portrays Christians as intolerant and oppressive. We get angry at things that frustrate our values.

In sum, then, according to Carter and Minirth, anger is an attempt to preserve our personal worth, needs, and convictions. By getting angry, we are communicating that something or someone has violated our personal boundaries.

Such a conceptualization is helpful for those of us who would like to get angry less often. We see through this framework *exactly* what needs to change in us: we have to find some way to reduce the size of these boxes that lead into anger. For example, to shrink the "essential needs" box, we could, as detailed in chapter 2, adopt a servant's mind-set. When we shift our focus from our needs to the needs of others, we'll have little or no expectation that our personal needs will be met. We are therefore less likely to be angry when our needs eventually go unmet.

Looking at the "disrespect" box, we may almost be able to eliminate it by deciding not to care what anyone but God thinks of us. If we can remain secure and joyful in the knowledge that we matter to God, we will be less offended when someone does not recognize our personal worth. It really doesn't matter what they think. If God approves of what I'm doing, who cares that someone else disapproves?

The point is that regardless of the circumstances or the behavior of others, we can do things unilaterally to reduce our propensity toward anger. However, we will still get angry at times—especially in our jobs. Then what? How do we typically respond when aggravated by our boss? Let's look at what the experts say about how we express our anger.

The Five Ways We Express Anger

In and of itself, anger is not necessarily good or bad. We know from passages like Eph. 4:26 that it is not a sin to be angry. Paul says here, "In your anger do not sin." He doesn't say, "Don't be angry." He doesn't say, "Anger is sinful and should be avoided." He tacitly acknowledges that this is a natural, human emotion and, accordingly, conveys that we need to be mindful about how we handle it.

As further evidence that anger is not sinful per se, consider the fact that Christ himself became angry in Jerusalem and cleared out the Temple as it burgeoned with deceitful merchants (Mark 11:15-17). It is a liberating scene for those of us who may otherwise feel guilty just because we are mad.

Returning, then, to the anger framework, it is clear that when we are angered by our boss, we have several options regarding what we could do with this emotion. The five general alternatives are defined as follows:

1. **Open aggression:** The *overt* preservation of personal worth, needs, and convictions at someone else's expense. Its intense form includes things such as rage, intimidation, ridicule, and blame. Among the more moderate forms of open aggression are insensitive criticism, sarcasm, and bickering.

2. **Passive aggression:** The preservation of personal worth, needs, and convictions at someone else's expense, but done in a quieter manner and with less vulnerability. Among the expressions classified as passively aggressive are complaining, sulking, pouting, evading others, gossiping, and covert misbehavior.

3. **Suppression of anger:** The refusal to admit that anger exists when in fact it does. The angry individual neither acknowledges the anger nor reveals it.

4. **Assertive but respectful response:** This more constructive release of anger entails the preservation of personal worth, needs, and convictions gently but persistently. One is considerate of others' interests and needs while simultaneously pursuing one's own.

5. **Drop it altogether:** One chooses to accept the circumstances or behaviors of others, to forgive, and to simply let the anger go. This differs from suppression of anger

because one recognizes that the anger exists and takes affirmative steps to remove it.[2]

OK. Enough theory. Let's see how this would actually work in practice. When we're mad at our boss, how do we use each of these five alternatives? When should we? What does the Bible instruct about each one?

An Openly Aggressive Response to Your Boss

"Don't be stupid," I was advised by a well-meaning colleague who was more levelheaded than I. "You might lose your job. At the very least, you'll make an enemy of the guy who decides your pay raises. Think about this over the weekend and talk to him on Monday."

He was right. Friday at 5 P.M. was no time to pick a fight with my supervisor. After innumerable days poring through résumés, checking references, and conducting interviews, I had finally identified one suitable candidate for our job opening. This person appeared to be a perfect fit. He not only was personable and funny but also really knew his stuff—the industry, our product, the customers' needs—everything. Moreover, he wanted the job badly. All systems said go. But my boss had vetoed the candidate without further comment.

"Why would the president of an organization micromanage a hiring process two levels below him!" I asked my friend incredulously. He never had done such a thing before. But now in one inexplicable swoop of his pen, he had perpetuated this nightmare search for the ideal middle manager. And I was livid. Without my sagacious friend there to remind me that I resided well below the president in the pecking order, I would have probably, in my haste, confronted him within minutes of hearing his decision.

For obvious reasons, we never explode at our boss. Rage and intimidation are not viable options for subordinates seeking recourse for unfair treatment. But other, more plausible alternatives also fall under the rubric of "openly aggressive," since this term is broadly defined as overtly preserving one's personal worth, needs, and convictions at someone else's expense. The most prevalent of these options in the 1990s, and one that is worth addressing for at least a few minutes, is to take the dispute to court.

Filing a Lawsuit Against Your Employer

As discussed a bit in chapter 2, we live in a culture that is incessantly focused on the protection of individual rights at all costs. "Fight for your rights!" and "No justice, no peace!" are among the common mantras heard today whenever some misfortune occurs or when someone appears to be treated unfairly. The media's constant portrayal of almost every American as a victim entitled to recompense only reinforces and exacerbates this culture of litigiousness. As a result, among our first inclinations whenever something bad happens to us in life seems to be the consideration of what rights we have, to what extent these rights have been violated, who's responsible for that violation, and how we can even the score with them.

This mind-set, when coupled with the low-cost legal options that are available (e.g., you only pay the lawyer if you win; a government agency will pursue the case on your behalf for free), has led to a recent explosion of lawsuits, especially suits contending some wrongful action by employers. According to the Equal Employment Opportunity Commission, formal allegations of workplace discrimination increased almost 50 percent in the first half of the 1990s.[3] But independent of our specific legal rights, we Christians must first ask, "Is going to court within the parameters of conduct laid out in the Bible?" More specifically, is it appropriate, according to Scripture, for a Christian to go to court over unfair treatment by the boss?

This is a hotly debated topic in many Christian circles; however, we need not spend an inordinate amount of time on it here because God's guidelines are reasonably straightforward.

Clearly, we must first be mindful of the very plain language of 1 Corinthians. Paul instructs in chapter 6, that Christians should settle disputes with each other outside of secular courts. Indeed, he goes so far as to say it is better to be wronged and cheated than to have unbelievers judge our disputes (1 Cor. 6:7). For this reason, organizations such as the Christian Conciliatory Council, Reconciliation Mediation, and the Christian Mediation and Arbitration Service exist to provide an alternative venue for adjudicating conflicts among Christians.

However, a dispute with one's employer is arguably another story. No such black-and-white prohibition exists in Scripture (except, of course, if one's employer is a church or other Christian organization, in which case the 1 Corinthians principle would seem to apply). Without explicit instruction here, we therefore need to consider *implicit* teachings on invoking rights.

Again, let's look to Paul. Paul had quite a tumultuous career as an evangelist, and it got him in more than his fair share of scuffles. He was accused, beaten, and jailed repeatedly, but interestingly, he seldom exercised any of the legal rights he had. In Acts 22, though, we do see Paul rely on the Roman law *in his defense*. He asks, as he's about to be whipped, "Is it legal for you to flog a Roman citizen who hasn't even been found guilty?" (v. 25). In doing so, he avoided an unjustified beating.

So Paul did rely on the law to defend himself. But throughout the New Testament we never see him counterattack. There is no record of him using the law to have his persecutors judged or jailed, notwithstanding that he, a Roman citizen, enjoyed greater legal protections than did the noncitizens who so often abused him. His choices along these lines, when we juxtapose them with Christ's familiar, radical teachings on turning the other cheek and offering a shirt to someone who has taken our coat (Matt. 5:39-40; Luke 6:29), give us pause regarding the propriety of legal recourse against our employer for things such as discrimination, privacy violations, sexual harassment, or inequitable compensation. At the very least, it seems, we must conclude that suing our employer for unfair treatment should be used *only as a last resort* after we have exhausted all other options. Although we may not be absolutely precluded from litigating unfair treatment, we will more likely be on firmer scriptural ground when we travel the "assertive but respectful" and "drop it altogether" paths discussed later in this chapter.

A Passively Aggressive Response to Your Boss

After suffering some mistreatment at the hands of our boss, it is much more common for us to express our anger in a passively aggressive fashion. Here, we are preserving personal worth, needs, and convictions at someone else's expense but doing it in a way that leaves us less susceptible to retribution. We express our anger, for example, by complaining, gossiping, or engaging in some sort of behind-the-scenes misconduct. We've already dealt with gossip in chapter 2, so let's look briefly at the well-traveled roads of complaining and covert misbehavior.

Complaining

Why waste time talking about something so innocuous as complaining? Everyone complains at one time or another. Sure, some people complain more than others, and yes, it can be a bit annoying at times, but really, what's the big deal? Isn't this a better way to release our anger than exploding, raging, and litigating?

These are reasonable questions, but here's a better one: "What does God think of complaining?" Does *He* think it's no big deal? Does *He* consider it innocuous? The Old Testament contains a sad, even tragic story that plainly illustrates God's perspective on our grumbling.

The Book of Numbers is not high on peoples' list of most beloved books of the Bible. In fact, many who have tried to read God's Word from cover to cover, if they are actually able to surmount the obscure terrain of Leviticus, have abandoned the effort entirely when confronted with something so mundane as the taking of a census in the first chapters of Numbers. And that's a shame for a plethora of reasons, not the least of which is that they'll miss some critical teachings on complaining in Num. 13 and 14.

In Numbers, Moses had just delivered the Israelites from Pharaoh's bondage, and they were on the verge of entering the Promised Land. When they reached the border, Moses sent 12 scouts into Israel to spy out the land, its resources, and its people and to report on the prospects of conquering it. Upon their return, 10 of the 12 related discouraging news: the land was indeed flowing with milk and honey, but the cities were fortified by large walls, and the people were numerous, large, and strong. These 10 concluded that there would be no way to avoid annihilation if they attempted to take the land.

However, 2 scouts, Joshua and Caleb, offered a different perspective, advising that the Israelites should trust that God would lead them to victory since He promised them the land. For this, the people contemplated stoning Joshua and Caleb and, instead of following the Lord into battle, elected to complain about Him and about their plight. "Why is the LORD bringing us to this land only to let us fall by the sword?" they grumbled, exasperated by the ordeal (14:3).

God was displeased to say the least. He threatened to send a plague to destroy most of them but then relented, selecting a different punishment.

"Punishment? Punishment for what?" we might ask. Verse 27 makes this clear as God asks rhetorically, "How long will this wicked community grumble against me? I have heard the complaints of these grumbling Israelites." Then in response to the complaining, He hands down His divine verdict:

> In this desert your bodies will fall—every one of you twenty years old or more who was counted in the census and who has grumbled against me. Not one of you will enter the land I swore with uplifted hand to make your home, except Caleb son of Jephunneh and Joshua son of Nun (*vv. 29-30*).

Thereafter, for almost 40 years, this community of several hundred thousand wandered in the desert until the generation of complainers died out.

To some of us the punishment may not seem to fit the crime. Forty years for misuse of one's tongue? It simply doesn't seem to be that flagrant an offense. In fact, for many of us today, complaining doesn't even register as a tepid sin. However, we must, as always, attempt to think as God thinks and be mindful of the central lesson from Num. 14: *God does not want us to complain about our circumstances.* Instead, He desires for us to be patient, to trust that He has a plan, and, in doing so, to demonstrate to others what it means to be Christlike. This is poignantly articulated by Paul in Phil. 2:14-15, where he writes, "Do everything without complaining or arguing, so that you may become blameless and pure, children of God without fault in a crooked and depraved generation."

Accordingly, we are to reject the cultural norms of our organizations that sanction and even encourage complaining as a legitimate response to workplace injustices. Rather, we are to be faithful to God's directives and seek His superior alternatives for expressing the anger we feel toward our boss.

Covert Misbehavior

Another common way we passively release our anger at work is to unilaterally pursue justice without our boss ever knowing about it. We find a way to get even simply by engaging in negative, behind-the-scenes workplace behaviors. To understand this alternative, consider the situation of our friend Mark. He feels that he has been treated unfairly—that his performance evaluation was inaccurate, that he is now underpaid, and that someone less deserving was promoted—and he now has a variety of options to regain some of what he rightfully deserves without the boss ever knowing about it.

Organizational psychologists, who research human behavior in organizational settings like workplaces, have for decades examined how we typically go about this. Among their many useful paradigms, they have long advanced something called Equity Theory to explain both how we ascertain that we've been treated unfairly and our likely response to such treatment.

In its simplest form, Equity Theory says that (1) fairness is important to people, (2) inequity is uncomfortable and creates a need to restore equity, and (3) people use a work-reward ratio to determine how fairly they're being treated and how they can even the score. The first and second pillars are sort of obvious: we care about being treated fairly, and if we're not treated fairly, we desire to do something about it. The third requires some elucidation.

Basically, part 3 of the theory contends (and much research confirms) that an employee looks at what he or she offers to the company versus what he or she gets back and compares this ratio to some other person's work-reward ratio. What we offer to the company—our "inputs" in Equity Theory jargon—include our skills, education, training, time, effort, and so on. What we get back—things like pay, benefits, status, prestige, a title, the size of our office or work space, and preference for shift assignments—Equity Theorists refer to as "outcomes." The comparison we make looks like this:

$$\frac{\text{my inputs}}{\text{my outcomes}} = \frac{\text{other person's inputs}}{\text{other person's outcomes}}$$

The other person in the equation could be just about anyone, from the person at the next desk to someone in another department to a brother-in-law who doesn't even work in our firm. The important part, though, is that to determine whether we are being treated fairly, we evaluate our work-reward ratio against someone else's. So if we have the same education, skills, abilities, and effort as another person (i.e., we have the same "inputs"), but that other person is being paid more (i.e., receiving a greater outcome), then we are likely to perceive unfair treatment. Similarly, if we are being paid the same as the next person on the assembly line, but we've been with the company a lot longer and bring to our job a lot more experience, we again are uncomfortable with the situation. In both cases, the work-reward ratio is not equal, so we tend to seek some way to "restore equity."

Applying this to Mark, we can be reasonably certain that he considers his colleague's promotion as tremendously unfair because not only does Mark view his own input to the company as greater (Mark has been there one more year than has his colleague), but on top of that, this less senior employee is now receiving a much greater outcome from the company (higher status, more compensation, more respect, etc.). The equation is completely out of balance, so the theory predicts (and common sense strongly suggests) that Mark will be very uncomfortable with the situation and will feel a need to somehow restore an equitable balance. *And here's where the covert misbehavior comes in.*

Mark could, for example, do what many in his situation would contemplate: decrease his effort. In equity terms, he's reducing his input to reestablish equilibrium in the formula. In plain English, though, he's saying to himself, "They're going to pass me over for a promotion? They're going to underpay me? Well, I'll just give them what they're paying for!" Period. Equity restored. Crisis averted. No explosive rage. Mark would be passively releasing his anger over this injustice by quietly cutting back on his contribution.

Or he could seek some way to increase what the firm gives to him. He's already been told he's not getting a raise, so he might respond by finding a way to increase his compensation on his own—without anyone knowing about it. Thinking "they owe it to me," Mark might begin to pilfer office supplies or catch up with friends and relatives on the company's long-distance bill or abuse the company credit card on his next business trip. Mark's work-reward ratio then starts to look more like that of the guy who got the promotion, affording Mark some feeling of vindication. Equity has been at least partially restored.

We can rationalize just about anything when we've been treated unfairly, but it goes without saying that this is not the scriptural approach. How we often respond in these situations bears little resemblance to how we should respond.

And how is that? Perhaps the most direct instruction that is on point can be found in Rom. 12. Paul, in verses 17, 19, and 20, says, "Do not repay anyone evil for evil. . . . Do not take revenge, my friends. . . . On the contrary: 'If your enemy is hungry, feed him; if he is thirsty, give him something to drink.'" If that were not enough, Paul's next statement makes him really sound like a bona fide nut case and is especially stinging to anyone who has encountered unfair pay, promotion, scheduling, or evaluation practices: "Do not be overcome with evil, but overcome evil with good" (v. 21). In other words, Mark's response to not being promoted and to getting no raise could be to work even harder. As difficult as this might be at that moment, he could refocus on the directives of his real Boss, his real Evaluator, and then repay the "evil" of an unfair promotion with the "good" of industriousness.

God's unconventional approach may not comport with our common sense; nevertheless, we are often called to do just the opposite of what Equity Theory predicts we will do.

Suppressing Your Anger at the Boss

Many people simply will not admit to anyone that they're angry. Some don't even admit it to themselves. When we refuse to recognize that we are angry and continue to go about our business as if nothing were bothering us, we are suppressing our anger.

People do this for different reasons. Some feel that all anger is bad and therefore never show it, choosing instead to hold it all inside. Psychiatrists tell us that many such individuals were raised in environments where an authority figure discouraged or invalidated the emotion—that a person is in essence trained to think that the emotion is evil or not normal. Others who suppress anger believe, very pragmatically, that no good can come from being angry and they see no point in expressing it, so they sweep it under the rug. The problem is, of course, that it is still under the rug. For this reason, psychiatrists generally agree that suppressing one's anger does nothing to eradicate it.

Along these lines, Drs. Carter and Minirth liken suppressed anger to moss living in a dark corner of a basement: you don't see it, but it's growing. And over time, there's a good chance that anger will produce adverse emotional and physical effects. Accordingly, although suppression may not be the worst way that one can deal with one's anger at the boss, it is considered neither a healthy nor desirable alternative.

However, such alternatives—practical, time-honored, scripturally sound alternatives—do in fact exist. It is to these that this chapter now turns.

A Biblically Based Response to Unfair Treatment

Scripture, as we've seen, offers a multitude of prescriptions that render the openly aggressive, passively aggressive, and suppression avenues deficient to varying degrees. Scripture also, not surprisingly, offers prescriptions for responding to mistreatment from our employer. A biblically based approach—essentially an amalgam of the "assertive but respectful" and "drop it altogether" alternatives—is presented below in four steps.

Step 1: Don't Resist or Immediately Respond

My friend Sal, a reasonably devout Christian, recently had a run-in with his boss. Sal was clearly the next in line to move out of a cubicle and into an office that boasted an impressive view of the city. Along with the office came natural light, privacy, and respite from the office chaos just by closing the door.

Seniority dictated rewards and entitlements in all areas of the firm: compensation, promotions, schedule preference, and so on. And it had always been used as the sole criterion for one's exodus from "cubeland." Now, with the imminent departure of an office resident came Sal's long-awaited opportunity.

He told me that all day on Wednesday, while awaiting the official nod from the powers that be to relocate his stuff, he had been humming "Movin' on Up," the theme song from the sitcom *The Jeffersons*. Sal had even identified the location of several sturdy cardboard boxes for the transfer of his books and files from his congested shelves. Then came the blow. Sal wasn't getting the office; instead, a female colleague, who Sal had seen flirting with the boss, was. New company policy: Offices will be awarded at the discretion of the boss. Sal was beside himself.

Point of decision. Whether one has a cubicle or an office with a view may appear completely trivial to many of us, but to Sal it mattered a lot. When he saw Colleen settling into his rightful place, Sal, in that instant, had a choice to make regarding how to deal with his anger. Unfortunately, such a potent emotion can confound one's better judgment, and in the heat of the moment, we do or say things that we later regret. So it was with Sal as he promptly stormed to his boss's naturally lit desk, demanded an explanation, and brashly insinuated wrongdoing.

Not smart. And certainly not scriptural. But all of the Scripture verses, biblical principles, and poignant sermons Sal had absorbed to that date were dominated by his anger. Even his normally reliable common sense couldn't save him. He responded in knee-jerk fashion with open aggression and, consequently, was later penalized for it.

A dispassionate examination of this event leaves us shaking our heads. Why would anyone respond so tactlessly? Who in their right mind yells at the boss? When we think back on our own lives, though, most of us can easily recall a time when we did something just as foolish. Perhaps it didn't happen in the workplace, but we let anger control us and later wished we hadn't. Injustice visited us and we threw objectivity to the wind. We responded instinctively. Quickly. Verbally. Probably improperly. Such a response is a function of the way we're made.

James spoke to this issue of our impetuous nature, offering a timeless admonition:

> When we put bits into the mouths of horses to make them obey us, we can turn the whole animal. Or take ships as an example. Although they are so large and are driven by strong winds, they are steered by a very small rudder wherever the pilot wants to go. Likewise the tongue is a small part of the body, but it makes great boasts. Consider what a great forest is set on fire by a small spark. The tongue also is a fire, a world of evil among the parts of the body. It corrupts the whole person, sets the whole course of his life on fire, and is itself set on fire by hell (3:3-6).

Our tongues get us in at least as much trouble as any other part of our body. James warns us here that they can be like a vehicle out of control, leaving a woeful path of destruction in their wake. He then goes on to relate the fatalistic news in verse 8 that "no man can tame the tongue." However, this does not relieve us from our obligation to put some reins on it. Christlikeness entails being "quick to listen, slow to speak and slow to become angry" (James 1:19).

When confronted by some type of unfair treatment at work, then, the lesson of James 3 (and Rom. 5, and 1 Thess. 5, and many other places in Scripture) is to avoid an immediate reply, as difficult as that may be, and to distance ourselves from the situation. That is, *the first step in responding to unfair treatment is to tighten the reins on our tongue and initially retreat.* Then, while taking refuge, we must do something that may be even more uncharacteristic in such situations: we must follow the Master's example and get on our knees.

In the Garden of Gethsemane, the One who was facing the most unfair treatment ever perpetrated fell to His knees and spoke to His Father. He did not run, He did not hide, He did not instantly seek counsel or invoke His rights. Anguished, He prayed, first that the injustice may pass Him by, but then that the Father's will be done, despite the fact that it might culminate in His death. Jesus' response to the pending travesty began with a retreat and a conversation with God.

Along similar lines, King David was in exile because his son Absalom had turned against him. Ps. 55 affords us some trenchant insight into David's fear, his anger, his grief, and the alternative responses with which he wrestled. David first contemplates *flight* writing, "Oh, that I had the wings of a dove! I would fly away and be at rest—I would flee far away and stay in the desert; I would hurry to my place of shelter, far from the tempest and storm" (vv. 6-8). In the next verses, however, he entertains notions of a *fight,* with God as the avenger: "Confuse the wicked, O Lord, confound their speech, for I see violence and strife in the city. . . . Let death take my enemies by surprise; let them go down alive to the grave, for evil finds lodging among them" (vv. 9, 15). Finally, though, David reconciles himself to the most appropriate starting point whenever confronting unfair treatment: trust God and have confidence that He is at work through this trial. He writes in verses 16, 17, and 22: "But I call to God, and the LORD saves me. Evening, morning and noon I cry out in distress and he hears my voice. . . . Cast your cares on the LORD and he will sustain you; he will never let the righteous fall."

David is now resigned to the promise that God will placate his trepidation, bringing him the inner peace he so desperately craves. And in doing so, David offers us the same lesson of Gethsemane: our first reaction to unfair treatment is not flight (i.e., quitting our job), not to fight (i.e., immediate open aggression), but to pray. At the critical moment where your emotions begin to consume you, at this definitive point of decision, select prayer as your first step to redress the wrong. It will be the turning point in this process.

Step 2: Reflect on Your Needs and Your Boss's Needs

It's at about this point that one might begin to dismiss this approach to overcoming unfair treatment as patently unrealistic. One might protest, "Are you telling me that when my firm ratchets up my workload by 20 percent because they're too cheap to hire more people, I'm supposed to just pray? Prayer won't get me home in time for dinner. Action will."

Prayer is only the first step in the process. It simultaneously affords God the opportunity to drain some of our anger, to offer us His wisdom, and to prevent us from doing or saying something we'd later regret. From here, though, unless God directs us otherwise, we begin to take action—assertively but respectfully. Christ himself advised us, "If your brother sins against you, go and show him his fault, just between the two of you" (Matt. 18:15). Clearly, it is entirely appropriate—arguably mandated—that we take action and address our boss directly regarding the decision or circumstance we perceive as unfair. Before broaching that topic with him, however, we should prepare a respectful response—a response that considers not only our needs but those of the boss as well.

Admittedly, this is tough. We don't care about our boss's needs at this moment. In fact, his needs are the last thing we want to think about. However, all of the teachings on servanthood, indeed Christ's living example of the principle, call us to persevere through this difficult task.

To effectively consider your boss's needs, begin with a list of the possible reasons *why* your boss may *really* have made the decision that angered you—in this case, why he increased your workload. You recall the reason that he gave to you, but there may be underlying factors involved as well. Put yourself in his shoes and think about what these factors might be.

Hypothetically, let's say your list looks like this:

- He needs to stay within the budget and could not afford to hire more help.
- He does not have the time to recruit and hire more help for the department.
- He is responding to the demands of his boss, who insisted on this solution.
- He knows that there are only a few people in the department that he can count on in a crunch, and you're one of them.

From this list, you can now ascertain the specific needs that must be met by any alternative solution you present to your boss: it cannot go over budget, it cannot require too much time to implement, it must satisfy your boss's boss, and it must ensure that the work gets done right. Many solutions may satisfy these interests. Your boss has chosen one of them, taking the position that your workload should be increased.

Thus, your strategy here, well-articulated in books such as *Getting to Yes* by Roger Fisher and William Ury,[4] is for the moment to forget about the boss's actual decision (i.e., his "position") and instead to focus on his needs that led to the decision in the first place. In doing so, you may identify other possible solutions to his problem that meet not only his needs but your own as well. Focusing on individuals' needs rather than on their stated positions is elemental to crafting a solution that satisfies and serves all parties involved. And it is the centerpiece of any "assertive but respectful" approach to addressing unfair treatment.

So let's assume that you conclude the real issues here are money and time: your boss can't afford another $25,000 a year in salary and $10,000 more in benefits for a new hire, and because he's too overworked, he doesn't have the time to investigate alternative resolutions to the workload problem. By uncovering his core interests in this situation, you may now be in a position to satisfy these needs in a way that doesn't entail increasing the workload (thereby satisfying your own needs as well). Hiring temps or independent contractors alleviates the benefit burden; moreover, it does not permanently increase the size of the department, so any budgetary strain may be temporary. You may therefore have another possibility to satisfy the boss's financial concerns.

But don't stop there. If you're going to make such a suggestion, go the extra mile and get some estimates for him. Do the groundwork for hiring someone by making a few phone calls. Identify what might be the best price in advance of your meeting with the boss to alleviate some of his burden in this process. In doing so, you may very well remove a stumbling block to the viability of this solution. You have saved your boss much of the time required to implement your solution.

The point here is basic. Before you set foot in the boss's office to address the injustice you perceive, consider the other side of the issue. Try to put away your anger at this person for the moment, identify his needs to the best of your ability, generate several options that will meet both those needs and your own, and carry some of his burden in the process. Although this tactic doesn't guarantee a solution to your problem, it is a respect-laden approach that could maximize whatever chance you have of redressing the unfair treatment.

Step 3: Respond with Gentleness

It's now time to respond verbally. If you're like I am, though, the greatest obstacle to accomplishing your goal here is not your boss, but yourself.

For many of us, civility is not necessarily our forte after we have been wronged. Although we may know intellectually that we must keep our emotions in check, as soon as we lay our eyes on our oppressor, the guy who just dumped another truckload of files on our desk, our commitment to this lofty teaching mysteriously absconds, and our old nature takes control. I recently crossed paths in the men's room with a colleague whose subjective, shortsighted evaluation of my work deprived me of a several thousand dollar bonus. While exchanging brief pleasantries with him, all I could think of was giving him a good piece of my Christian mind.

Such thoughts can sound the death knell for an assertive, respectful, scriptural approach to our problem. All of our effort to this point will be for naught if we do not, when engaging the boss, contain our emotions and respond in gentleness.

Webster's dictionary defines *gentle* with such words as "polite, generous, kind, tame, serene, patient, and meek." It is an attribute that is clearly embodied in the person of Christ. Jesus was gentle in the face of all kinds of potential adversity: when preaching a new doctrine, when run out of His hometown of Nazareth, when admonishing His disciples, when He stood before the Sanhedrin, when He faced death before Pilate, and countless other times. So, too, we are called to personify gentleness throughout our lives, but especially during its most contentious moments. Phil. 4:5 is illustrative, directing Christians to "let [their] gentleness be evident to all," and 2 Tim. 2:24 reinforces the principle instructing that "the Lord's servant must not quarrel; instead, he must be kind to everyone, able to teach, not resentful." Similarly, Paul tells Titus to "remind the people . . . to slander no one, to be peaceable and considerate, and to show true humility toward all men" (Titus 3:1-2). Gentleness is indeed the hallmark of a Christian.

However, God does not simply proclaim our duty to be gentle without also assuring us of its value. In the Old Testament, we learn that "a gentle tongue can break a bone" (Prov. 25:15). In the context of our discussion here, this means that there are ways to break our boss's bones that are preferable to the traditional "openly aggressive" techniques. Stated a bit more seriously, expressing our concerns gently may gain us swifter recourse than will our more instinctive approaches.

Another benefit of gentleness is found in Ps. 34:12-13 where David writes, "Whoever of you loves life and desires to see many good days, keep your tongue from evil." That is, a gentle disposition in everything we do is the vehicle to a happier life—in and out of the workplace.

Most Christians know such things implicitly, but it is still the exception for us to actually apply this principle on the job. In this sometimes despotic environment, we easily rationalize "an eye for an eye" because it is the cultural norm, thereby turning our backs on the entire new covenant. But God doesn't provide loopholes. He permits no exemption for those of us employed by a curmudgeon. Instead, the Lord counsels us that when we finally confront our boss about unfair treatment, regardless of what he's done and regardless of how he responds to us, gentleness is to be our modus operandi.

Step 4: Patiently Endure While Working to Drop It Altogether

Now let's say, hypothetically, that the boss denies your appeal to return your workload to a level that is humanly achievable. He flatly refuses to consider augmenting the staff in any way, and he doesn't seem to care that you now have a lot less time for your family. He simply retorts matter-of-factly that the industry has gotten so competitive that we all have no choice but to bear some hardship. Then he gives you a pep talk about being a good team player and doing your part.

You seemed to have done everything by the Book to this point. You initially backed off, you prayed, you considered the boss's needs and sought ways to meet those needs, you approached the subject privately and gently in his office, and you bit your tongue when he scoffed at your suggestions. And for all of this effort, you lost the battle. Miserably. It wasn't even close.

Time to complain or sulk or enjoy more extended trips to the watercooler? Time to confront the boss? Not exactly. Rather, it's time to apply one of the most excruciating principles in Scripture: it's time to patiently endure a trial.

An "assertive" response is one that persistently seeks to preserve our personal worth, needs, and convictions. However, it by no means assures us that those things will in fact be preserved—immediately or ever. And for those of us who tend to be impatient, we are tempted at this point to throw up our hands and say, "Enough is enough!" The openly and passively aggressive responses are looking pretty attractive right now—especially since it seems that everyone else is traveling those routes.

But God calls us to resist and, furthermore, to patiently endure. And here is the place where so many Christians seem to recoil. We drop the ball at this point because God is simply not making any sense. We have been faithful to Him and have tried to obey the rules. In fact, we've been pretty good by most humanistic measures. And now He rewards us with hardship? This seems like nothing short of betrayal! After all we've done for God, why have we become recipients of His wrath? It's completely unfair for Him to ask for patience.

But consider this: isn't this exactly the attitude of many children with respect to some of their parents' actions? Don't children resist just about any form of discipline at the time it is administered? We know that parents discipline their children out of love for them—to shape them, mold them, and train them to behave properly. It is, in fact, for the child's own good. We know these things. So why is it so difficult to accept that our Heavenly Father may be doing the same thing for us?

Let's face it, we Christians are not all that Christlike. We fall light-years short of His perfect standard. To usher us toward that standard—to shape us and train us—the Lord sometimes uses suffering. It's not a punishment, although we may choose to see it this way, but an instrument of love used for our greater good.

Patient endurance of trials develops in us attributes that make us more Christlike. First, it gives us a greater ability to gracefully overcome life's storms. They are inevitable and numerous, as they were for Jesus himself, and we can learn to cope with them properly only through experience. Just as a good workout makes us stronger for the next one, so, too, patient endurance of trials increases our capacity to endure.

We also develop a more earnest reliance on God through this process. When we examine our hardships in retrospect and see how God did indeed come through for us and maybe even changed us for the better, we are that much more confident during our next bout of suffering that God is there with us and that He'll come through again. Having seen this process come to fruition, we now trust Him and depend on Him more than we did before. Patient endurance bolsters our dependency and our faith.

In short, God is building Christian character within us. As we persevere through trials, our persona can be transformed to more closely resemble Christ's. And when this happens, it precipitates something miraculous: *our perspective on everything in life changes.* As we are sanctified and begin to see the world through the eyes of Christ, burdens seem less burdensome, daily irritants seem less irritating, unfair treatment seems less unfair, persecutors seem less sinister, personal needs become less important, and our fears and anxieties abate. And into this vacuum rushes *hope.* As we start to at long last embrace the principles of the Beatitudes, we gain a confident expectation about the future, about our ability to handle anything life has in store for us. Moreover, with our faith fortified, we gain greater hope for eternal salvation. This is the chain of events Paul speaks of in Rom. 5 where he boldly asserts that "suffering produces perseverance; perseverance, character; and character, hope" (vv. 3-4). It is out of love—out of a desire to give us hope—that God permits suffering in our lives. As with a woman in labor, from something overwhelmingly painful comes a blessing of unspeakable proportions.

This is why Scripture makes the seemingly bizarre claim in several places that we are to rejoice when suffering comes our way. Most notably in James we do not get more than two verses into the book before encountering this truth. James says hello in verse 1, and then in his quintessential, no-nonsense fashion, immediately presents one of the most exacting tasks in all of Scripture:

> Consider it pure joy, my brothers, whenever you face trials of many kinds, because you know that the testing of your faith develops perseverance. Perseverance must finish its work so that you may be mature and complete, not lacking anything (1:2-4).

. . . As Christ was mature and complete, not lacking in anything. Suffering produces perseverance, which sanctifies us and gives us hope. For this reason, we are to "give thanks in all circumstances" (1 Thess. 5:18), including those times when our jobs and our bosses make our lives miserable. God is working here, shepherding us down a path that will ultimately culminate in real relief from our burden: the ability to accept our circumstances as they are and to drop the anger we feel toward our boss.

Dropping our anger is the last footprint on this long, agonizing journey. We see this instruction conveyed to the Ephesian church as Paul writes,

> Get rid of all bitterness, rage and anger. . . . [And instead, be] kind and compassionate to one another, forgiving each other, just as in Christ God forgave you (4:31-32).

But when you think about it, is it *really* possible to forgive your boss and to just "get rid" of your anger? Probably not if we stubbornly adhere to our conventional responses to workplace injustices. Certainly not if we have allowed our hardship to engender bitterness and resentment. However, if we've patiently endured, heartened by the knowledge that God is trans-forming us, if we've truly "set [our] minds on things above, not on earthly things" (Col. 3:2), no boss's behavior is insurmount-able. No managerial decision is unforgivable. In fact, *seldom* will we be ruffled by the subjective decision making that is so preva-lent in organizations.

Instead, the fruit of patient endurance—a changed heart—will enable us to consider this workplace matter against the backdrop of eternity, to put it in proper perspective, and to firmly believe that "our present sufferings are not worth com-paring with the glory that will be revealed in us" (Rom. 8:18). Thankfulness for God's "indescribable gift" (2 Cor. 9:15) will supplant any bitterness we harbor, paving the way for gen-uine forgiveness. And then, by God's grace, the anger will be gone.

When things do not go our way at work, when we are treated unfairly or get some other raw deal, we have the op-tion to patiently endure the outcome, allowing God to mature us and to help us drop our anger. Even when we cannot find justice in the workplace, through Him we can always find so-lace.

A Brief Application: Dealing with Unfair Pay Practices

Before closing this chapter, let's recap by applying its mod-el to the commonplace scenario of unjust compensation.

Very few people would describe themselves as overpaid. And not many more would say they are paid what they're worth. Because one of the central reasons we work is to sustain ourselves economically, the structure and equity of our firm's compensation practices is a touchy and sometimes volatile sub-ject for us.

And the subject comes up a lot. In fact, inequitable pay has been so intrinsic to the human experience throughout history that Jesus used it to construct a parable about the most impor-tant of all topics. Recall the story of the workers in the field from Matt. 20? To illustrate that it's never too late to gain eternal life, Jesus told of a vineyard owner who paid all of his workers equally, even though some had worked many hours and others had worked few. My guess is that Jesus selected the analogy of inequitable pay to make this vital point because people throughout time could easily identify with it. Such treatment at work existed before the birth of Christ, while He walked the earth, and ever since. It has been a timeless point of reference for all generations, so we should not be surprised when it visits us as well.

Applying the framework described in this chapter, we become angry about unfair pay for all three reasons in the model. First, and most obviously, because we need money to survive, unfairly low pay inhibits our ability to provide for ourselves, our families, and others. An essential need is going unmet, leading to anger. Second, we all feel some conviction that people should be paid equitably. If the person next to us, who has been doing the same job the same way for the same period of time as us, is paid more, that doesn't seem fair. If they get a larger bonus at Christmas, we'll probably perceive a glaring injustice. Here a personal conviction is being undermined, igniting our wrath. Third, because we are indoctrinated by our culture to correlate pay level with one's personal worth, the higher our pay, the more other people might respect us. How many times have we heard some well-paid acquaintance casually let slip his or her salary in a transparent effort to gain our respect, admiration, or awe? Compensation that we perceive as unfair disrespects us and fuels our anger.

So we're angry about our pay because we seek to preserve our personal worth, needs, and convictions. And because we're dealing with money, this anger is often intense. We can express it "openly aggressively" (angrily confronting the boss, suing the company, etc.), "passively aggressively" (complaining, reducing our effort, covertly stealing things because the company "owes us"), or by "suppressing" it (pretending it doesn't bother us). A biblically based approach, however, entails first stopping to think and to pray about the issue. One could contemplate, for example, why he or she is so upset about, say, not getting a bonus. Speaking with God about this may lead us to identify whether our own greed or pride are really at the root of the problem here. In the opening scenario, Mark wanted a raise to buy luxuries and wanted a promotion to have an impressive title. Prayer and reflection, even talking with a trusted Christian friend, might assist him to see this more clearly. Before he ever responds to his boss, then, he may conclude that he should be content with his current pay and position. In this light, it may not be difficult for him to immediately "drop it altogether."

If our anger is not a function of our sinful nature, though, we can then progress to step 2 and begin to juxtapose our boss's needs with our own. Perhaps there are some legitimate competition-based constraints. Or maybe the boss is simply responding to someone above in the bureaucratic hierarchy. Bosses seldom allocate compensation arbitrarily, so before broaching the topic of unfair pay with your boss, attempt to identify the needs that underlie the decision and think about alternative ways that these needs could be met.

Step 3 is to respond gently, as Christ would. Be persistent, seek to satisfy your interests through a private meeting, and maintain your composure and your diplomacy. If you are denied what you are requesting and if this denial is rendered in an impolite or insulting manner, keep your emotions under control. Remain in close touch with the Lord throughout these anxious moments, and He will give you strength.

Fourth, patiently endure any resolution that does not go your way without resorting to subversive behavior. Continue to work hard, mindful that what you're being paid, either in absolute dollars or relative to others, has nothing to do with your motivation or your productivity. As discussed in chapter 4, we work first and foremost for the Lord and should produce accordingly. Patiently suffer through this unfair treatment and attempt to rejoice that the Lord is shaping you in the process.

Finally, work to drop the anger you feel. Patient endurance will ultimately give you the capacity to evaluate this injustice in the context of all of the gifts in your life—and especially in the context of eternity. See this trial for how frivolous it really is in the whole scheme of things, and then forgive your boss. Even the most horrible treatment fades from significance when compared to the glory that is ours in the afterlife.

If all of this sounds oversimplistic, let's dismiss any such pretense once and for all: responding in this manner, for many if not most of us, will be one of the most arduous endeavors of our lives. Everything within us and everything we are told by our culture, our coworkers, and sometimes even our well-intentioned friends and family encourage us to respond carnally.

In fact, when the whole world is acting one way, God's approach to dealing with unfair treatment seems unattainable and almost absurd. "Pray? Meet my oppressor's needs? Be gentle and kind? Be patient? Forgive and let it go? Give up my right to be angry and to secure what I deserve? Who has ever done it that way!"

Christ has. And with His assistance, you can too.

Conclusion

That evening, Mark lay in bed staring at the ceiling. As the day's events refused to let go of his mind, his thoughts drifted back to a business course he took in college. He had a vague recollection of the professor rambling on about some guy named Caleb who had been passed over for a promotion by God around the time Moses died. Mark got out his Bible and reacquainted himself with the story.

Of the 12 men sent into Canaan to scout out the Promised Land, only Caleb and Joshua encouraged the Israelites to trust God and go into battle. For this, both were blessed decades later as the only men of their generation to enter Israel. Mark skipped to the Book of Joshua and read that God selected Joshua as Israel's leader. "Why not Caleb?" Mark thought. "He had been just as faithful as Joshua. He was almost stoned for his scouting report. Why was Joshua promoted instead of him?"

As Mark continued through Joshua's memoirs, he traversed the celebrated account of Jericho and later, in chapter 14, reencountered Caleb. Now 85 years old, when most people would be packing it in, what was this spurned servant up to? Caleb was asking Joshua to assign him the land in Hebron so that he could drive out the Anakites.

Anakites. That looked familiar. Mark flipped back to the story of the 12 scouts in Num. 13 where he had been a few minutes earlier and saw again that the Anakites were the hill people—the giants—the people who were so large that they scared 10 otherwise faithful men out of trusting the Lord. And now at age 85, Caleb, the guy who was passed over by God, the guy who was arguably slighted, the guy who would never have the glory of Joshua and would certainly never have his own book of the Bible, was responding to his Boss's rebuff by requesting to take on the biggest bullies in the neighborhood. At age 85 nonetheless! He wasn't bitter. He didn't complain. Quite the contrary, he was rolling up his sleeves, putting his faith in God, and seeking another Jericho experience.

Mark needed to read no farther. He had all the instruction he re-

quired to deal with his situation. The appropriate response to being passed over for this promotion was for him to redouble his effort and do an even better job over the next year.

———·———

Unfair treatment hurts. It violates us, it undermines our dignity, and it leaves tremendous bitterness in its wake. It is certainly among the most difficult things at work to address from a Christian perspective because the cost appears to be so high. What if God's approach doesn't remedy the injustice? What if I don't get what I deserve by doing it God's way? What happens if God doesn't come through the way I want Him to?

We Christians ask a lot of silly questions and do a lot of impulsive things when we're not thinking clearly. And we're seldom thinking clearly at the moment that we react to mistreatment by our boss. This is why it is essential to commit to memory the following familiar verse and to have it at our instant disposal on the job. It has for millennia assisted people to make the right choices in times of trouble.

> Trust in the LORD with all your heart and lean not on your own understanding; in all your ways acknowledge him, and he will make your paths straight *(Prov. 3:5-6)*.

Through His Word, the Lord has blessed us with an effective mechanism for addressing and overcoming workplace injustice. To tap into its power, though, we must first courageously resist leaning on secular advice or our own instincts and instead wholly rely on God's approach, even when a lot is on the line—and especially when a lot is on the line. He will come through for us, He will make our paths straight, if we will trust Him.

6

Balancing Work and Family

MICHELLE STOOD AT THE BAY WINDOW, *staring out into the neighborhood. With each passing set of headlights, she grew a little more impatient. She wasn't worried that something had happened to Mark; 12- to 14-hour workdays had become pretty standard over the past several years. She was just a bit lonely and anxious to see her husband. After briefly returning her eyes to the television, she heard a car door close.*

"Hi there, stranger!" Michelle greeted him with a cheery grin. "You want some dinner?"

Mark returned a warm but sagging smile, dropped his briefcase, and removed his tie. "Already ate," he said. "But thanks anyway. I missed the kids again, didn't I?"

*"Well it **is** 9:30. Ryan colored this picture for you, though. I told him you'd hang it in your office."*

Admiring the multicolored scribbles, Mark sadly shook his head. This was the third day in a week he hadn't seen his son at all. And his six-month-old daughter seemed to barely know who he was. He peeked into the nursery and then stepped into Ryan's bedroom. "He's getting so big," Mark thought to himself as he adjusted Ryan's blanket and kissed him on the head. "Where is the time going?"

"Can I at least fix you a snack?" offered Michelle as Mark returned.

"Thanks, but I'm absolutely beat," he replied, glancing at the mail on the kitchen counter. "And I've got to catch a plane at 7:00. I just need to turn in."

———-———

For millions of people every day, this unhappy scenario is nonfictional. With only so many hours in a day, the more we spend at work, the fewer we have for our loved ones. It's a zero-sum game that's not much fun to play.

Balancing work and family responsibilities has been a challenge ever since God commanded Adam to work in the Garden of Eden. Did you ever find it interesting that in that very same chapter of Genesis, God gave him a wife? Within a few little verses Adam transitions from a life whose most arduous task is watching new trees grow, to having both a full-time job and a full-time spouse. Welcome to the world, son. Here's a shovel and a wedding ring!

The proximity of these two biblical events, I would suggest, foreshadowed the timeless juggling act that would be inherent to humankind. The Lord created work and family in the same breath, and His first instructions were for us to attend to both. Hence, the tension. How much time and energy do we devote to each? Does one have priority over the other?

Indeed one does. The Scriptures speak generously to the eminence of marriage and family in both the Old and New Testaments. Beyond Genesis, and most notably, Christ himself put His full weight behind the sacred nuptial union, underscoring that husband and wife are to become one flesh, that nothing should separate them, and that divorce is almost always prohibited (e.g., Mark 10, Matt. 19). These are not simply disposable relationships, He teaches us; rather, marriage and family are absolutely central to the Lord's blueprint for civilization. Accordingly, for these God-ordained institutions to be protected and nurtured, we must respect the priority of family over work as well as over all our other earthly endeavors.

For Christians, this is a no-brainer, though. We know this to be axiomatic. Still, many of us do not heed it. Notwithstanding the directives of the Bible, for many the only place where family comes before work is in the dictionary.

And the problem seems to be getting worse. According to a large 1994 study by researchers at the University of Maryland, parents now spend an average of 17 hours per week with their children, down 40 percent from 1965.[1] Parents, however, are not necessarily comfortable with that. Sixty-six percent of more than 3,300 adults recently surveyed by the Families and Work Institute, a nonprofit research group in New York, said they wanted more time with their kids.[2] A lot of children are uneasy with this situation too. In 1996, Gary Bauer's Family Research Council reported results from a children's poll indicating that almost one in three children ages 8 to 12 say that they do not spend enough time with their fathers.[3]

Many variables contribute to these numbers, but prominent among them is the sacrifice of family for job and career. This sacrifice, of course, is not always by choice; sometimes we see no alternative but to compromise family time. After all, a family needs to eat. It needs to have a roof over its head. And more generally, we continually need to respect the unambiguous admontion of 1 Tim. 5:8: "If anyone does not provide for his relatives, and especially for his immediate family, he has denied the faith and is worse than an unbeliever." Financial need certainly constrains many of us to spend more time away from home than we'd like.

Related is the issue of job security. Some of us are employed in jobs where if we do not put in the required, oppressive number of hours, we'll soon be unemployed. As a result, for the sake of the family, we are often physically absent from them.

However, *some Christians have indeed made a choice—consciously or not—to permit work needs to dominate family needs.* Why would someone choose such a lifestyle? For some, it is because work provides a much-needed escape from the exhausting obligations of homelife. Anyone who's a parent—especially the parent of young children—knows that one's job can, in fact, be much less physically and emotionally demanding than life at home. The *real* work, according to these folks, takes place on the weekends and in the evenings. Consequently, their credo has become, "Thank God it's Monday!"

For others, the culprit is a basic human need for self-esteem. We all have an intrinsic desire to feel that we matter, that we're important and valuable. And when nothing on the home front seems to meet this need, most of us find something else that will. Sometimes that "something else" is another person, and other times that void is filled through investing inordinate amounts of time in one's career, tallying ego-boosting achievements.

Relatedly, some people (actually many people) choose work over family simply because they are engaged in the incessant quest to conquer the world—to gain power, status, money, possessions, and the admiration of others. Because the reward structure in most organizations is such that one rises faster and higher if one works 80 hours a week, pursuit of these prideful or greedy objectives—even the seemingly noble pursuit of securing many luxuries for the family—often entails making some wrong choices with respect to family time. These choices may appear rational and defensible when they are first made but later in life reveal themselves as abysmal, even tragic decisions. Most of us have known at least one "successful" individual who has late in life regretted slighting family to ascend the corporate ladder.

Besides the possibility of a few regrets, though, what is the earthly price of permitting work to come before family? Is it really that exorbitant? Consider briefly just a few of the effects on marriages and children directly attributable to such choices.

When Work Is a Higher Priority than Your Marriage

Not too long ago a friend of mine confided in me that he and his wife were experiencing a bit of an estrangement. I can't say that I was exactly shocked. For years Kent had been on the road at least as much as he was home. It was simply part of his job as a sales representative. And on the days that he *was* in town, he seldom returned from work without plenty to keep him occupied. He loved his wife, there was no doubt in his mind about that, but she was becoming increasingly aloof. Whereas they once had little trouble talking late into the night, now they seemed to have almost nothing to discuss and only a few common interests.

"Katie's been working a lot too," he told me. "More now than ever. And she's stopped hinting at having kids. Doesn't even want to practice at it, if you know what I mean. I guess we're just growing apart."

I would hasten to guess that this conversation, in various forms, takes place thousands of times every day. And I would further conjecture that the vast majority of the problems are rooted in the same things: failure to nurture the marriage and treat it as a top priority in one's life. If you don't water a plant, it will wither and eventually die.

Kent and Katie were growing apart because, in large part, they stopped trying to grow together. They plainly and simply were not spending enough time together and had long abandoned their attempts to meet each other's needs. The work-family imbalance may have caused the problem, or it may have just been a symptom of a broader problem, but that was now immaterial. If Kent permitted the imbalance to persist, it would operate like a choke hold on his marriage.

Donald Merideth, in his book *Becoming One*, describes four steps to the decay of a marriage: Romanticism, Reality, Resentment, and Rebellion.[4] Twenty-something Kent slid rapidly through this very progression. A few weeks after our initial conversation on the subject, we had a second, significantly uglier one that started something like this: "Mike, I know what you're gonna say, but I've just got to tell somebody about this! I met the girl of my dreams at work. She's unbelievable—a new trainee right out of college, and . . ."

Pathetic. Kent was now in open rebellion and embarking on a sordid affair whose story line would read like something from daytime TV: frequent trysts; an unwanted pregnancy; an abortion; a suspicious wife who hires a detective; a desperate, last-ditch attempt at reconciliation; and ultimately a highly contentious divorce.

Placing work ahead of marriage does not guarantee infidelity, but it sure produces some fertile ground for it. Many people reading this know it to be true from painful, firsthand experience; others can glean the connection directly from Scripture. Writing to the church at Corinth, for example, Paul warns married couples not to allow anything to wedge itself between them—neither work nor children nor anything else—and to avoid extended periods of emotional or physical separation "so that Satan will not tempt you because of your lack of self-control" (1 Cor. 7:5). Permitting work to be an interloper in one's marriage fuels temptation.

It can then fuel sin as we, like Kent, acquiesce to that temptation. When someone experiences perpetual discontentment at home, the workplace can quickly become the enemy's playground. It is here that we have many close friendships with members of the opposite sex. It is here that we share with co-workers common trials that have the curious effect of bonding us. And it is here that we usually see people at their most attractive. For those who travel on business, the temptation becomes even more intense. There's nothing like a lonely hotel room in

Atlanta to get some unhappily married person's mind wandering.

But whether or not working too much culminates in adultery, couples who sacrifice marriage for career often find themselves before a judge. Indeed, the highest divorce rates in America exist among those whose careers are just starting to take shape: for men the highest rates exist in the 30-34 age-group, and for women it is the 25-29 range.[5] Failure to keep spouse and job in proper priority invites at best a lackluster marital relationship and quite often, as the marriage unravels, a broken home and a broken life.

When Work Is a Higher Priority than Your Kids

In his humorous but insightful book, *Fatherhood*, Bill Cosby writes,

> There is no commitment in the world like having children. Even though they will drive you to consider commitment of another kind, the value of family still cannot be measured. . . . This commitment, of course, cannot be a part-time thing. The mother may be doing ninety percent of the disciplining, but the father still must have a full-time acceptance of all of the children. He must never say, "Get these kids out of here; I'm trying to watch TV." If he ever does start saying this, he is liable to see one of his kids on the six o'clock news.[6]

There's a poignant truth in that wit. How many kids bum around the neighborhood or roam our town and city streets with nothing to do after school? How many children, even in two-parent homes, are starving for attention and seeking self-esteem in all the wrong places through all the wrong behaviors? Far too many. And the lion's share of the problem traces its roots, again, to the number of hours we invest in our jobs and, more broadly, to our frenetic pace of life.

What is the effect of this lifestyle on a child? James Dobson, considered by many to be America's foremost family counselor, writes in *Raising Children*,

> The inevitable loser from this life in the fast lane is the little guy who is leaning against a wall with his hands in the pockets of his blue jeans. He misses his father during the long days and tags around after him at night, saying,

"Play ball, Dad!" But Dad is pooped. Besides, he has a briefcase full of work to be done. Mom had promised to take him to the park this afternoon, but then she had to go to the Women's Auxiliary meeting at the last minute. The lad gets the message—his folks are busy again. So he drifts into the family room and watches two hours of pointless cartoons and reruns on television.

Children don't just fit into a "to do" list very well. It takes time to be an effective parent when children are small. It takes time to introduce them to good books—it takes time to fly kites and play punch ball and put together jigsaw puzzles. It takes time to listen, once more, to the skinned-knee episode and talk about the bird with the broken wing. These are the building blocks of esteem, held together with the mortar of love. But they seldom materialize amidst busy timetables. Instead, crowded lives produce fatigue, and fatigue produces irritability, and irritability produces indifference, and indifference can be interpreted by the child as a lack of genuine affection and personal esteem.[7]

What a shame when this happens. And how counterscriptural this lifestyle. Ps. 127 counsels us, "Sons are a heritage from the LORD, children a reward from him. Like arrows in the hands of a warrior are sons born in one's youth. Blessed is the man whose quiver is full of them" (vv. 3-5). God, through Solomon, instructs that we are to treat our children as a *reward and a blessing,* not as a burden, not as one more thing to do among all of our other duties in life, and not as something of equal importance to our work. They are a divine gift, and we are charged to nurture them as such.

One person who appeared to have some difficulty applying this truth was Solomon's father. The life of King David demonstrates that even an exceptional CEO who is "a man after [God's] own heart" (1 Sam. 13:14) can completely screw up his family. Although David's name has become synonymous with giant killing, effective military leadership, and adultery, his story also affords us some critical work-family lessons in the area of child rearing.

David was a guy who seemingly spent entirely too much time at the office. The Book of 2 Samuel tells us that during the first 20 years of his reign, between the ages of 30 and 50, he was an overwhelming success, conquering thousands and bringing tremendous economic prosperity to Israel. But then in the second half of the book, we learn of several family debacles. His son Amnon commits rape, and David does nothing about the crime. After 2 years of David's inaction, another of his sons, Absalom, takes justice into his own hands and murders Amnon. Absalom then turns the nation against David, sending his father into exile. Such a calamitous sequence of events implicates family neglect: the failure to instill godly values in children, the failure to reprove their sinful behavior, and the failure to cultivate a loving, respectful child-parent relationship. David, it seems, may have been too preoccupied with his work to treat his children as a reward, spend time with them, and train them properly. Consequently, he reaped the tribulations that are sown by parental indifference.

The central lesson here is that a child's position in his or her parents' pecking order of priorities is *the main determinant* of that child's growth and development. You can be remarkably successful in the workplace, surmounting the middle-management ceiling, accumulating extraordinary wealth and possessions, garnering the veneration of the world, and even doing beneficent things with your treasures. But if you're not attentive to the home, when you later search your quiver, you may find the arrows blunt, warped, or missing altogether.

Tips for Striking a Better Work-Family Balance

For the exhausted person who is attempting to juggle these many balls, what's the answer? The starting point, I would suggest, is to step back and take an inventory of your life to ascertain if an imbalance between work and family life indeed exists. Which has first priority? As one measure, for the next few weeks keep some mental notes regarding what's on your mind when you're at work versus when you're at home. Do you find yourself thinking more about your work while you're at home than you do thinking about your spouse and kids while you're at work? If so, it may indicate inverted priorities. As another measure, ask your spouse, your kids, your close coworkers, your other friends, and anyone else who might be able to offer an objective opinion on the matter whether they think family comes before work in your life. Listen to them carefully without arguing, and then prayerfully weigh the evidence to establish whether an adjustment is warranted.

Some people have this priority mastered. For the rest of us, though, after undertaking this introspective study, we'll need to proactively respond to strike a better work-family balance.

To shift that balance back to family, step 1 is to make a commitment to God that our life priorities will be God, then family, then work. Making such a commitment is pivotal because it prompts us to take this lifestyle modification seriously. It compels us to forge ahead, to earnestly pursue this, and to persevere when it inevitably becomes inconvenient. Making this promise to God is a watershed event that will undergird and perpetuate this difficult transformation.

Having made this vow, there are then several affirmative steps we can take to keep us on the correct path:

Be Accountable to Your Spouse

Nationally renowned counselors Gary Smalley and John Trent, in their book *Love Is a Decision*, furnish us with a simple yet effective technique for keeping spouse and work in proper priority. Smalley writes of the turning point in his marriage:

> I actually began to prioritize my life from zero to ten, zero being something of little value, ten something of highest value.
>
> I established God and my relationship with Christ as the highest—a ten. On a consistent basis, I began looking to my spiritual life and asking the question, "One to ten, where is my spiritual life with Christ?" "How highly do I value His Word?" "Prayer?" "Sharing my faith?"
>
> Then I placed Norma above everything else on this earth, way up in the high nines. With this relationship, too, I often asked myself (and Norma), "How am I doing at making you feel like you're up in the high nines, above every one of my hobbies and friends and favorite sports teams? What can I do to keep you believing you're a high nine?"[8]

For many people, conceptualizing issues—even relationship issues—in numeric terms is useful. Quantifying the relative priority of our spouses (something that Smalley and Trent call the honor quotient) and regularly asking our spouse to evaluate it constructively acts as a check against permitting other things in our life to become more important. If we have historically allowed work or hobbies or even children to take precedence over our marriage, being accountable to keep one's spouse feeling like a "high nine" minimizes the chance of backsliding into our old way of doing things.

Think in Terms of Presence, Not Presents

Many people work an incredible number of hours so they can give their families the best of everything—the best house, the best food, the best clothes, the best toys, the best education, the best car, and so on. Meanwhile, they neglect to offer the best of themselves. In addressing this topic with the wife of a man who worked feverishly so he could buy luxuries for his family, Billy Graham in *Answers to Life's Problems*, wrote,

> It is surprisingly easy for some men (and women) to fall into your husband's trap, without ever really thinking about or realizing how illogical it is. For example, if you were to ask most of them why they work so diligently to give their families financial security, they would say it is because they love them. But they fail to see that never spending time with their children and spouse (as well as working themselves into an early grave) is the most unloving thing they can do.
>
> Your husband needs to readjust his priorities. Yes, he has a responsibility to provide financially for his family. But he also has a God-given responsibility to provide for the emotional and spiritual welfare of his family—and he cannot do that if he is totally preoccupied with money and things.[9]

It is one thing to work extra hours to buy necessities, it's quite another to voluntarily choose additional work time for indulgence sake. When faced with the option to work more than is required, never forget that your family needs your presence more than they need your presents.

Provide Both Quality and Quantity Time

All too often parents permit themselves to work excessively under the assumption—the dangerously fallacious assumption—that the *quantity* of time left for their kids does not matter as long as there is *quality* in the time they actually spend with them. Let me again defer to James Dobson's *Raising Children* for the best analogy I've ever heard illustrating the folly in such reasoning:

> Let's suppose you are very hungry, having eaten nothing all day. You select the best restaurant in the city and ask the waiter for the finest steak in his menu. He replies that the filet mignon is the house favorite, and you order it charcoal-broiled, medium rare. The waiter returns twenty minutes later with the fare and sets it before you. There in the center of a large plate is a lonely piece of meat, one inch square, flanked by a single piece of potato.
>
> You complain vigorously to the waiter, "Is this what you call a steak dinner?"
>
> He then replies, "Sir, how can you criticize us before you taste that meat? I have brought you one square inch of the finest steak money can buy. It is cooked to perfection, salted with care, and served while hot. In fact, I doubt you could get a better piece of meat anywhere in the city. I'll admit that the serving is small, but after all, sir, everyone knows that it isn't the quantity that matters; it's the quality that counts in steak dinners."
>
> "Nonsense!" you reply, and I certainly agree. You see, the subtlety of this simple phrase is that it puts two necessary virtues in opposition to one another and invites us to choose between them. If quantity and quality are worthwhile ingredients in our family relationships, then why not give our kids *both*? It is insufficient to toss our "hungry" children an occasional bite of steak, even if it is prime, corn-fed filet mignon.
>
> Without meaning any disrespect . . . my concern is that the quantity-versus-quality cliche has become, perhaps, a rationalization for giving our kids *neither!* This phrase has been bandied about by over-committed and harassed parents who feel guilty about the lack of time they spend with their children. Their boys and girls are parked in child care centers during the day and with baby-sitters at night, leaving little time for traditional parenting activities. And to

handle the discomfort of neglecting their children, Mom and Dad cling to a catch phrase that makes it seem so healthy and proper. "Well, you know, it's not the *quantity* of time that matters, it's the *quality* of your togetherness that counts." I maintain that this convenient generalization simply will not hold water.

To guard against falling into this trap, it is useful to set aside some *nonnegotiable time* to be with your family every day. Make it your personal policy to be with your kids for, say, two or three hours each workday. And rigidly stand by it. Consider this time when nothing else can be scheduled. Creating such a policy for yourself will have the effect of constraining your work life to meet your home schedule, rather than the more typical converse. For certain, there will be those days when, because work takes you out of town or because there's a deadline fast approaching, you must make an exception, but these days should be rare.

Relatedly, because mealtime is so integral to family bonding and growth, make it your goal to average two meals per workday with your family. Again, during some weeks this will be impossible, but most of the time the goal is attainable.

Lastly, do not work on the Sabbath. This, of course, is not simply a personal policy option that creates more home time, it is a biblical mandate. It is a practice by which we honor the Lord and our family simultaneously. But what if your boss requires Sabbath work? Stand firm. Answer no. It simply is not within the realm of possibilities because God has proscribed it. And if this threatens your job? The law protects you, somewhat. As long as accommodating your religious needs does not impose more than a minimal cost on your employer, under law adverse action cannot be taken against you.

If Necessary, Cut Back on Work Responsibilities

Making more time for family means compromising time somewhere else in life. We've been saying in this chapter that if work is consuming the majority of your waking hours, this is the logical place to compromise.

"But, time out here!" some will protest. "Cutting my work hours means either cutting my responsibilities, working faster during the time I do have at work, or reducing the quality of my work. I'm already working as fast as I can, and if I consider my work as something to honor God, I can't sacrifice quality. That leaves cutting responsibilities, and if I do that, my career will stagnate."

Those who have control over the amount of work they perform (an arrangement enjoyed increasingly by white-collar and blue-collar folks alike) will eventually face some hard choices. Once we vow to shift our priorities, we may find that the only way we can be faithful to that vow is to simplify our work lives, to back off some of the projects, to forgo the promotion, and indeed to subordinate our career aspirations to family needs. The Lord calls us to put our pride and ambition and greed on a shelf, candidly forewarning us that "a greedy man brings trouble to his family" (Prov. 15:27). Putting family first, therefore, entails confronting our carnal desires and willfully making whatever career sacrifices are necessary.

Ask God for Help

Never forget that the Lord is your ally in this endeavor and that He wants you to succeed. While you're on your knees making that vow we discussed earlier, ask the Lord to guide your thoughts, your words, and your actions. Ask Him to help you overcome your sinful nature so that you can see clearly to make the right choices. Return to this prayer regularly, and He will shepherd you to a victorious new lifestyle.

Conclusion

That Sunday morning, Mark, as always, sat in the fourth pew with his family. As he waited for the service to begin, he perused the bulletin to see what this week's message would be. From the sermon's title, "Coming Home," Mark thought the congregation would be treated yet again to an invitation to turn their lives over to Christ. As the sermon unfolded, though, Pastor Thompson's preaching instead targeted Mark's current trial.

Whether it was the pastor's eloquence on the value of family, his citation of divorce statistics, or his anecdotes about people whose families had disintegrated because career was their idol, something resonated with Mark. He knew it was time to make a choice — God's choice.

Later that day, Mark took his family to the park for a picnic, and

...ying grace, vowed to the Lord and to his family that no matter
...is priorities would change.

———··———

If there is one thing that Christian employees need to consider daily, it is the extent to which work time displaces family time. It's often laborious to ponder—and even more exacting to address—perhaps this most difficult element of applying Christianity in the workplace. But failure to remain vigilant in this area can have dire consequences.

Without a doubt, making family a higher priority than work entails sacrifice. You'll have to make some career adjustments. You may have to get off the fast track, work less overtime, or even find another job. You'll have to overcome pride, ambition, and greed to resist the lure of power and money. In all likelihood, you'll probably earn less income than you would otherwise. The Christian approach to this issue comes at a price.

But it also comes with a promise—the promise of a richer life. Those who are willing to align their definition of success with God's definition will be blessed with a happier, more stable marriage. They will enjoy a closer relationship with their children and will have more time to train them up. In their later days, they will reflect on innumerable fond memories and have few regrets. Indeed, they will count themselves among the richest people in the world.

7

How to Be a Great (and Godly) Boss

I WISHED THIS DAY would never come," Mark thought to himself as he perused his list of subordinates. The list—more of a spreadsheet, actually—detailed the experience, education, performance reviews, seniority, and salary of each employee for whom Mark was responsible. Now, in the face of corporate-wide downsizing, he was required to undertake the agonizing task of shortening this list.

For the hundredth time this week, he turned his eyes to the performance column. And for the hundredth time, it was clear that two individuals were obvious candidates for the axe. Most of Mark's subordinates were assiduous, highly skilled, fresh-out-of-grad-school types who contributed real value to the firm. Martin and Denise, however, were not so exemplary, their productivity lagging far behind their peers. If two people needed to be cut, they were the logical choices.

But this was a lot more complicated than ranking individuals by performance. Martin was the sole breadwinner for a large family. With two kids in college, three others in the pipeline, and a hefty mortgage, losing this job could be disastrous. Moreover, at the age of 53 he would have few prospects for other employment that would pay his bills.

Denise's case seemed even more problematic. A single mother of three grade school children, she often arrived late, left early, and was unavailable on weekends. Her lackluster productivity was almost solely a function of her family responsibilities, but she was without doubt the lowest performer in the group. How could Mark possibly fire a single mother?

But how couldn't he? If she stayed, someone twice as productive had to go. Life was a lot simpler before his ascension to the corner office.

———

"Why does a business exist?" the Wharton professor asked the class of about 100 M.B.A. students. "What is its central objective?"

Perplexed about why he was asking something so patently

obvious, the students initially responded with nothing but silence. Was this a trick question? Maybe he was just asking rhetorically.

When it soon became clear that the professor did not intend to answer his own question, one student tersely offered, "To maximize profit?" This, of course, was the launch point the professor sought, and on this common assumption—one that elicited no dissent in this venue—the class set off to explore competitive strategy in the global marketplace.

From day one in business school, and from day one in our for-profit corporations, we are indoctrinated to think in terms of maximization of shareholder wealth. The inculcators tell us to pursue single-mindedly greater market share and return on investment, to ensure high quality and customer satisfaction, to improve productivity and efficiency, and to contain costs. Intellectual heavyweights from Adam Smith to Milton Friedman have unabashedly (and often convincingly) advocated neoclassical economic perspectives of the firm, asserting that the only ethic that matters and the only social responsibility of the firm is to increase profits. Period. End of business ethics discussion.

With respect to the management of our subordinates, then, this paradigm implies that whatever a boss does—recruitment and selection of employees, orientation and training, evaluation of performance, compensation, relocations, job design, scheduling, layoff and termination—organizational performance is the lone touchstone. Nothing else should influence the managerial decision-making process.

But what's wrong with making money? Even from a Christian perspective, there is nothing inherently sinful about profit. In fact, the Old Testament is replete with anecdotes of the Lord blessing individuals with prosperity. We do know as Christians, though, that contrary to the contentions of the neoclassicists, the business lobbyists, countless CEOs, consultants, and smarter-than-thou business faculty nationwide, the story does not in fact end with profit. The Lord has His own theory of the firm, offering timeless wisdom on both the role of a business and how one can be a great boss. This chapter looks to His management text to extract some basic principles for managing people and for overcoming our reluctance to adopt this unorthodox approach. It then offers more specific guidance on how to manage people in a manner that satisfies both scriptural and shareholder mandates, and it closes with the story of the ServiceMaster Company, a 4-billion-dollar firm that has successfully implemented scriptural principles throughout its history.

A Basic Framework for Ethical Decision Making

What should that M.B.A. student have said in response to the professor's question? Any answer other than the one he offered would have surely led to suspicions regarding his professional potential and perhaps made him a target for a semester's worth of inquisition from the front of the room. But if Christ was sitting in the third row and He raised His hand, what would His response have been?

That's not a question we particularly enjoy dealing with because we know the answer will be so inconvenient. Of course Christ would say that we have a broader responsibility as business people, as managers, and as owners than to generate and stockpile green paper. He would probably contend, to a chorus of frowns, eye rolling, head shaking, and snickers, that as with everything else in our lives, we should "set [our] minds on things above, not on earthly things" (Col. 3:2) and that in business, therefore, our primary objective should always be to please our Father in heaven. He would dispense with all conventional wisdom and teach that *for the Christian, the purpose of a business and the central aim of a boss should be to glorify God.*

This does not mean one ignores profit, He might soon add for this audience. Absent this pursuit, no one will have a job in this firm or benefit from its product or service for very long. However, the pursuit of profit is to be a *means* and not an *end* in business. Profit is one of several vehicles by which the Christian businessperson honors the Lord in his or her work.

The intricate task of the Christian boss, then, is to always keep one eye on the bottom line and two eyes on scriptural principles. To illustrate, consider again the layoff scenario. Mark's been directed to reduce the size of his department. Firms that are restructuring typically do so borne of a need to cut costs, to improve efficiency, and to effectively respond to competitive pressures. Reliance on individual conscience or any other subjective criteria is often strongly discouraged by top management in such situations.

As a Christian, though, Mark's first responsibility is not to top management, but to God. In all dealings of consequence with his employees—hiring, firing, compensation, and so on— he must attempt to do so in accordance with biblical minimums. Therefore, while he is clearly to be mindful of that performance column, he also has a duty to look far beyond it and ask, "What would the Lord have me do here?"

For some people, pictures help to clarify concepts. Mark's options, graphically depicted in Figure 7-1, can be conceptualized as adjacent, partly overlapping circles. The left circle represents all possible decisions that would appear justifiable from a profit perspective. Included would be every alternative that enhances his department's long-run performance, some of which seem ethical from a Christian standpoint, others which do not. The right circle includes all those decisions that appear to comport with the Lord's will as revealed by Scripture.

Points A, B, and C, then, represent three distinct options. Point A would be an option that likely increases profits but cannot be defended as scriptural. Arguably, point A might be something like terminating the underproductive single mother without offering her any other assistance. Point C, conversely, would be an alternative that seems to be in line with God's Word but does not take into account the firm's economic needs. Laying off some younger, highly productive employees and offering them a generous severance might be one of many such points near C.

However, the Christian manager, I would suggest, should actively avoid the A's and Cs of this world, and instead, seek the Bs: the options that satisfy both profit and scriptural directives. And contrary to the prevailing notions in corporate boardrooms, there are usually many possibilities in this intersection. I will touch on several later in this chapter, but for completeness of this discussion, I offer one here: Mark should lay off based on economic criteria such as performance potential but never, *never* do so before the targeted employee has found an equivalent job elsewhere. If the single mother is to be cut, Mark should wait until she's found something else to sustain her. If Mark thinks that will take too long, he should expedite the process by helping her find the job himself.

As detailed later, many alternatives reside in this intersec-

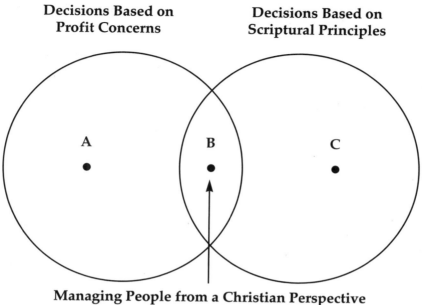

Decisions Based on Profit Concerns

Decisions Based on Scriptural Principles

Managing People from a Christian Perspective Entails Operating Within This Intersection

Figure 7-1

tion for all types of personnel issues. The challenge for the Christian boss is to identify and to implement them. To do so, though, one must first gain a foothold on what this scriptural circle entails for the management of people.

Scriptural Principles for Managing People

A dispute arose among them as to which of them was considered to be the greatest. Jesus said to them, "The kings of the Gentiles lord it over them; and those who exercise authority over them call themselves Benefactors. But you are not to be like that. Instead, the greatest among you should be like the youngest, and the one who rules like the one who serves? For who is greater, the one who is at the table or the one who serves? Is it not the one who is at the table? But I am among you as one who serves" *(Luke 22:24-27).*

Jesus Christ, indisputably the greatest Leader of all time, led by serving. Through example and through word, He taught the world what it means to be a godly leader. In deed, we see

Him wash people's feet, heal the sick, feed thousands, teach the people about the Father, raise the dead, forgive sins, and continually pray for us. Whatever people asked of Him, He did. In word, He taught this principle of servanthood, directly stating, for example,

- "If anyone wants to be first, he must be the very last, and the servant of all" (Mark 9:35).
- "Whoever wants to become great among you must be your servant, and whoever wants to be first must be your slave—just as the Son of Man did not come to be served, but to serve" (Matt. 20:26-28).
- "For everyone who exalts himself will be humbled, and he who humbles himself will be exalted" (Luke 14:11).

As the consummate Leader, He is the ideal Model for the Christian boss. Therefore, before we buy into any supplemental theories on leadership, some of which are decent, many others of which amount to mere psychobabble, we should commit to emulating His servant-leadership example.

But what exactly does this oxymoronic term, "servant-leader," imply in the workplace? What does it entail in a practical sense for a boss?

Boiled down to its essentials, servant-leadership turns conventional bureaucracy theory on its head, maintaining that *a primary objective of a boss is to meet the needs of his or her subordinates.* That is, servant-leaders identify and facilitate (1) what their subordinates require to reach their potential at work and (2) what their subordinates need to live a comfortable life. They are humble, relinquish their right to be king of the world, and instead consider it their job to carry burdens.

As I pondered on this point for the first time, a student asked me what appeared to be an innocent, elementary question: "So what exactly are these needs of employees that I'm supposed to meet?" I recall babbling through an answer, sounding confident enough to be convincing, but gradually realizing full well that the response was insufficient. I offered up the usual suspects—fair pay, a safe work environment, adequate time off, and other things—but proffered no coherent framework from Scripture. That experience prompted me to delve much more deeply into the Word to extract the following more informed (but, I think, still improvable) response.

It seems that all employee needs that are to be addressed by the servant-leader fall into two general categories: human dignity and familial obligations.

Human Dignity Needs

Recall from chapter 4 that the primary purpose of work is to glorify the Lord, to follow His example, and to thereby gain fulfillment as a human being. Each person is dignified as a child of God and is called to use his or her diverse talents to honor Him. Christian bosses must therefore respect this calling of their subordinates. And beyond that, they are to expedite this divinely fashioned arrangement. That is, it is the servant-leader's job not only to recognize the dignity of the people who work for him but also to protect and nurture it.

In practical terms, what does this mean? What are the specific implications for management policy? I would suggest several things:

- *The payment of a living wage.* This is not necessarily the market rate or the legally required minimum, but rather a wage that is governed by what an individual needs to live in reasonable and frugal comfort.

- *The provision of a safe and healthy work environment* and, relatedly, *the minimization of dehumanizing aspect of jobs.* Is it dignifying for someone to perform the same task for eight hours a day, five days a week? Do we give glory to the Lord by permitting noisy, smelly, oppressive conditions to persist in our manufacturing environments? Is it respectful to treat employees in an arbitrary or discriminatory manner? We may not be able to eradicate all of the negative conditions of our workplace, but we can usually do something to improve the job environment.

- *Employee participation in decision making.* Employee empowerment has been a hot topic for some time, almost to the point of becoming clichéd. But if implemented properly (as demonstrated in the appendix to this chapter, for example), it can enhance both dignity and performance. Many organizations continually solicit and implement employee ideas, allowing individuals even on the lowest level to participate in the restructuring of work, the streamlining of processes, the allocation of rewards, and the development of new products.

- *Personal and professional development.* Continuous job training is a primary vehicle by which workers can improve knowledge, skills, and abilities; augment their contribution; advance their careers; and realize self-worth. Few investments generate returns on so many dimensions.

- *Adequate rest.* Most workplaces have evolved to include periodic breaks, holidays, and vacations, but the parameters of rest periods are typically governed by legal or contractual minimums or by labor market forces. Time off should instead be a function of what people really need to restore their physical and mental strength and, as noted below, a function of family responsibilities.

- *Care for employees in times of sickness, old age, unemployment, and disability.* In the United States, we've established state and federal systems as a safety net in these areas, but are they adequate to meet the needs of your people? Will an illness or disability relegate your workers to a life of poverty? Will 700 bucks a month in social security be sufficient for your retirees? The only way to really know is to put yourself in their place for a moment, examine what type of lifestyle you would have to lead under these constraints, and then consider whether or not it is dignified.

Family Needs

As covered in chapter 6, the Bible speaks extensively to an individual's duty to family, thereby implicating a second category of employee needs. The powerful tutelage of 1 Tim. 5:8, for example, is representative: "If anyone does not provide for his relatives, and especially for his immediate family, he has denied the faith and is worse than an unbeliever."

In many cases, a supervisor, more than anyone else, controls whether or not an individual can effectively fulfill this directive. That is an *awesome* responsibility. The Christian boss, the servant-leader, is therefore called to be ever cognizant of employee familial obligations when making pivotal people management decisions.

Applying this principle would seem to involve the following:

- In addition to productivity, skill, experience, and other conventional variables, an individual's family needs should be considered when setting a wage or determining a salary increase. Servant-leaders should therefore consider employee family size, financial obligations, and other special circumstances when making pay decisions.
- In the same way, your employees must be able to fulfill their families' health needs either through employer-provided health insurance or by having adequate pay to purchase their own insurance.
- Sensitivity to familial obligations is also critical when considering requests for family leave or an accommodation for pregnancy and when determining issues such as who will be relocated to another state, which of two equally qualified candidates will be hired, and, indeed, who will be laid off.

Some Consequences of Meeting Employee Needs

Will attending to human dignity and family needs cost money? You bet. And plenty of time too. But servant-leadership is not necessarily about maximizing profit; it is about storing up treasures in heaven. According to evangelical Max DePree, former CEO of Herman-Miller Furniture, "The servant-leader is a servant first,"[1] and that means putting people before profit and thinking as Christ would think, independent of the cost.

However, a residual consequence of this approach to management, however, should be a *positive,* rather than a negative, financial return on this investment. The cutting-edge human resource research coming out of places such as Rutgers, Harvard, and NYU empirically demonstrates that these types of investments in people significantly increase profits through higher productivity and lower turnover.[2] Firms that operate this way, as described through the ServiceMaster story in the appendix to this chapter, gain a competitive advantage through effective management of their people.

Indeed, it is a radical paradigm to define a leader as one who serves, but it is in fact a Christian paradigm taught by the Master himself. And in light of this evidence that it may improve organizational performance, this technique for managing people seems to fall within the intersection of scripturally based and profit-based decisions. So why don't more Christian bosses practice it?

The Number One Obstacle to Servant-Leadership

Servant-leadership is a concept that is relatively easy to understand and one that many Christian bosses would have little trouble inferring for themselves from reading Scripture. So why do so few of them seem to apply it? Think back for a moment. How many of your bosses who have professed to be Christians have sought to serve your needs before meeting their own? The embarrassing answer speaks volumes about our resistance to walk our talk.

But what is the root of our reluctance? I would submit that for the vast majority of Christian bosses, the number one obstacle to adopting a servant's mind-set is not a failure to understand or interpret the Bible, but rather it is their own innate pride. Once we've invested years to gain the promotion to boss, we feel entitled to significant deference by our subordinates. Since we're now distinguished from them by rank, we presume that *it is their job to serve us,* that it is *their* responsibility to meet *our* needs. We command, they comply—this is the secular golden rule for the superior-subordinate relationship.

Reading about this servant-leadership principle can therefore be a bit disconcerting. To be a servant-leader means to forfeit the status conferred on everyone else who practices a more traditional form of people management. It is to give up our right to be the king or queen of our own little fiefdom. It is to do the unnatural and to choose humility over ego. Accordingly, to pursue God's will with subordinates, a Christian boss must start by conquering pride. But to do so, one must first understand it.

Pride has both a positive and a negative connotation. The positive type, to borrow from *Webster's,* essentially means "worthy self-esteem" or "delight or satisfaction in one's achievements, possessions, children, etc." For example, we are proud of ourselves after we graduate from school, get a job, or reach other milestones. We are proud of our parents, children, siblings, and friends when they achieve great things. We're proud of our local sports teams, of our church and pastor, and of our communities. We're proud of our work after painstaking labor gives way to eventual accomplishment of the task at hand. This type of pride is not sinful.

But the more common manifestation is a grievous sin. The sinful form of pride is defined as "too high an opinion of oneself; conceit; haughtiness; arrogance; and exaggerated self-esteem." It is a preoccupation with ourselves, a placing of ourselves at the center of the world and conceptualizing everything in the context of how it affects us. We see it in its rawest form in toddlers. Their attitude is, "Me, me, me, me, me . . . ," "I want . . . ," and "I need . . ." Little else matters. Life revolves around them, and when it doesn't go just their way, grab the earplugs.

In many cases, not much changes from ages 2 to 32 to 62. Our tantrums may be less frequent and less overt, but the attitude is still there. Problem is, we don't think it's a big deal, so we fail to correct the attitude or the consequent behavior. We continue to insist that the world revolve around our needs, even as adults. At home, we make unreasonable demands on our spouses and children. In the workplace, we think our subordinates should defer without question. "After all," we reason, infected by original sin and corporate culture, "I'm the boss!"

Wrong. God's the Boss. And He *does* think pride is a big deal. If you're inclined to disagree, check out that Tower of Babel story again (Gen. 11), almost any chapter of Proverbs, or Christ's repeated denunciation of the Pharisees. It is God's will for us to begin overcoming this carnally motivated self-worship *today* by putting Him at the center of our thoughts. Without this willingness, we will never be able to sustain the humility to be a servant-leader.

You may say, "I know that, and with an occasional slipup here and there, I'm a pretty humble boss." Some have indeed been blessed with such attributes, but to gauge where your footprints currently stop on this journey, consider this reality check from Dr. Richard Mayhue, vice president and dean of the Master's Seminary in California. He writes that true humility is marked by the following:

- Greater desire to serve than to be lord (Matt. 20:26-27)
- Peace with being last rather than first (Matt. 20:16)
- Contentment in living low rather than high (Phil. 4:11-12)
- More satisfaction in giving than receiving (Acts 20:35)

- A compulsion to forgive rather than to exact punishment (Matt. 18:21-35)
- A desire for exaltation only by the hand of God (Matt. 23:12)[3]

To what extent are these things true in your work life? Truth be told, few of us score very well on this index. And unfortunately, our score seems to decline the instant we receive a title and some subordinates. But the good news is that we're not waging a futile war—even those of us who have grappled with this sin for decades. The Lord promises you a humble servant's heart once you finally take the courageous, selfless step of asking for it. Along these lines, Ezek. 36:25-26 says:

I will cleanse you from all your impurities and from all your idols. I will give you a new heart and put a new spirit in you; I will remove from you your heart of stone and give you a heart of flesh.

Through this transplant, a procedure that will be divinely performed as often as you desire it, the Lord will pave the way for you to be an effective, successful servant-leader.

Some Practical Guidance for a Few Tough Issues

For those who desire a closer look at the inherent complexities of servant-leadership and how it is currently applied in some workplaces, we now turn to a few personnel issues that increasingly call supervisors to servanthood in the trenches: employee compensation, flexible work schedules, nondiscrimination, and layoffs and termination.

Employee Compensation Decisions

Here's a pretty straightforward question: how much should you pay someone to perform a job? Usually firms will develop a wage structure that uses industry average pay as a benchmark. Some will pay above market in an effort to attract the best and brightest and to retain their top performers; others will adopt the strategy of paying below market to keep costs down and to pass savings along to their customers. To set individual wages, then, firms consider not just the going rate for the job but, of course, the employee's education, skills, experience, effort, attitude, past performance, seniority, and a host of other "compensable factors." Moreover, most firms offer additional benefits (vacation, pension, health care, etc.) that currently average about 40 percent of payroll. So how much should the Christian boss pay?

In the abstract, we can think of a plethora of points that fall somewhere in the two circles of Figure 7-1, and perhaps a handful of those would simultaneously satisfy employee human dignity and familial needs while positively impacting organizational performance. But when you're attempting to reconcile tensions between financial realities and real human needs, the decision-making process is a lot murkier than can be captured by any paper model.

To illustrate some of these complications, consider this hypothetical situation. Let's say that you own a small restaurant, and every six months you meet with your subordinates individually to discuss the quality of their work, map out strategies for improvement, and let them know what their raises will be. In front of you now sits one of your cooks, Ron, awaiting your evaluation of his performance. As with most of your employees, he is doing an adequate job: nothing special but nothing wrong. Nobody has complained about the food, the guy shows up on time to work, and he has a decent attitude. You pat him on the back and raise his pay 5 percent, from $7.00 an hour to $7.35.

At this point, he nervously asks you to reconsider his compensation. He relates to you that his aging, widowed mother is in need of nursing-home care, something he cannot possibly afford on his salary. Also, with a new baby on the way, Ron's expenses will soon be growing, and further complicating his financial problems, his wife will have to take unpaid leave from work for several months. He asks you, quite contritely, to double his pay to $14 an hour, about $29,000 a year—more than any other employee is earning. What do you tell him?

For some people, this is easy. The answer is, "No. Get back to work." Can't afford it, can't create those type of inequities, can't be increasing people's pay every time there's a crisis in their personal lives. What is this, a business or a charity?

That's for you to decide. Christianity certainly conflates the two. As the owner, you could unilaterally decide to carry Ron's burden, regardless the cost, and do things such as give him a loan, offer him a financial gift, find him a higher paying job, or actually agree to raise his pay an unprecedented amount. And consequently, you might suffer some financial loss or create some morale problems in the process. But following the faith has its price, and if we never find ourselves paying it, we need to take a long look at whether we're indeed followers. My guess is that Christ would find some way to meet this employee's needs.

In general, though, based on the experiences of several organizations, I would take issue with the conclusion that carrying employee financial burdens adversely affects morale, turnover, performance, or profits. Many organizations have institutionalized this approach to compensation and have still remained competitive. Beyond addressing special employee needs on an ad hoc basis, the most common compensation practice of this genre is to provide an additional stipend for primary wage earners. For example, many Protestant elementary and secondary schools pay a "head of household" premium to male and female employees who earn more than 50 percent of the combined annual wage earnings in their household. Some for-profit Christian book publishers have done the same thing. Applying the same principle, J. C. Penney's department stores, founded by evangelical James Penney, who sought to always run his business on Christian principles, have historically offered additional health benefits to "head of household" employees. (By the way, if you're looking for a fascinating case study in Christian management, read *Fifty Years with the Golden Rule* by James C. Penney, Harper and Brothers, 1950.) Family need can indeed be used as a compensable factor in business.

Profit sharing is another compensation strategy that firms are increasingly adopting to put more money in employee pockets. Of course, the primary impetus for a firm's adoption of profit sharing is enhanced productivity, not family need, but this approach has manifested itself as a strategy that passes both shareholder and scriptural muster. Not only do employees often enjoy a large bonus at year's end (sometimes more than 100 percent of their base wage!), but also according to the best research to date, profit sharing has been demonstrated to boost productivity between 3.5 and 5 percent, with smaller firms realizing even larger gains.[4]

The point here is that there usually is some intersection of the profit and scriptural circles in the area of compensation. You can, in fact, have it both ways. There will be those exhausting times when the Ron's of this world challenge us to rethink our reward strategy, or even to do something unprofitable for the sake of glorifying God, but these are some of the extra miles we travel as Christian bosses.

Flexible Work Schedules

Earlier, when introducing servant-leadership, we briefly touched on an employer's responsibility to accommodate employee familial obligations when designing work schedules. Although some have traditionally protested that accommodation will inhibit efficient and effective completion of the work, many organizations have in fact successfully balanced these sometimes competing objectives without compromising either organizational performance or the principle of servanthood.

According to a recent survey by the Society for Human Resource Management (SHRM), the largest professional organization of human resource managers in the country, 46 percent of firms currently use something called flextime.[5] The flextime approach to scheduling creates a "core" of hours during which all employees are expected to be on site, typically 9 A.M. to 3 P.M., and permits employees to choose their hours around this core. In a typical flextime scheme, an employee must work 8½ hours (or sometimes 8 hours with a working lunch) and can begin as early as 6:30 A.M. Other approaches permit employees to work late on, say, Wednesday and Thursday, and then leave early Friday afternoon. Employees can therefore schedule their workday around family needs, traffic concerns, and any other personal issues that demand flexibility. Does it create productivity problems? Actually, most flextime firms continue to use the system because they reap the benefits of longer hours of operation without increased personnel costs and of more productive, more satisfied employees (because they are working at their most convenient, most productive times).

That same SHRM survey reported that about one in five firms permits some employees to "telecommute." In this age of electronic data transfer, many employees can work just as effectively (if not more so) from home and simply use the phone, fax, or modem to communicate with the office. Although this arrangement will not be tenable for every position, it is an increasingly employed accommodation for parents of young children and for children of elderly parents. And interestingly, the available research on the practice suggests that telecommuters put in longer hours than do their nontelecommuting peers because they're not in a rush to get home.[6] Working in a bathrobe may also have some positive effect on productivity, but that has yet to be investigated.

Another scheduling accommodation is the "compressed work week." As the name implies, this involves working the 40 or so required weekly hours in fewer than five 8-hour days. For example, many nurses work three 12-hour shifts each week. Some firms use a 4-40 system (40 hours in 4 days, with Friday or Monday off) or a 9-80 system (80 hours every 9 days, with the 10th day off). Presently, about one in four firms permits the scheduling of compressed work weeks.

Some miscellaneous family-friendly ideas from industry include the following:

- Allowing parents to take a child on business trips (25 percent of firms—some of whom pay for the child's trip)
- Employee sabbaticals (they're not just for professors anymore; 12 percent of firms permit these extended leaves of absence with one-quarter of these firms paying employees during their time off)
- Shortened summer hours
- Elder care on site
- A pretax transfer of funds to a flexible spending account for child/elder care (about 6 in 10 firms currently allow this)
- And boldly staking out the next frontier, some firms are permitting employees to bring their pets to work, provided they are properly house trained (the pets, not the employees!).[7]

There are indeed certain logistical, supervisory, and equity issues that inevitably arise when accommodating family obligations. But thousands of managers around the country can attest—and millions of their grateful subordinates will affirm—that such problems are dwarfed by the benefits of flexible work schedules and that the problems can be overcome to ensure that quality work is completed in a timely fashion.

Nondiscrimination

Anyone who has been a supervisor for even a short period of time knows that each managerial decision that affects employees entails navigation of the minefield that is contemporary employment law. In the United States, employees are now statutorily protected from workplace discrimination on the basis of race, color, sex, religion, national origin, age, union status, disability, and in some places, marital status, sexual preference, smoking habits, personal appearance, height and weight, political affiliation, arrest and conviction record, and even, in one state, the method of birth control they choose. Supplementing these federal, state, and local laws, courts in many states have permitted employees to sue their employers for wrongful discharge, a cause of action that safeguards workers from almost every other type of arbitrary or discriminatory treatment by their boss or company.

The primary rationale underlying all of this regulation is that an employer should be unbiased when making managerial decisions about applicants or employees. It is our public policy to minimize the use of pernicious managerial criteria.

One could certainly take issue with the pervasiveness of the regulation or with the necessity, value, or wisdom of certain laws; however, I would contend that in general, nondiscrimination is one of those personnel management areas that clearly falls in the intersection of profit-based and scripturally based decisions. It is relatively obvious how this affects the bottom line: it is not profitable to be paying attorney fees, court costs, settlements, and adverse judgments. Moreover, it is virtually impossible to operate while undergoing a discovery process from some federal or state agency. And don't forget the media: a few sexual harassment charges, meritorious or not, and you're front-page news, enduring a local or national boycott and repairing your public image for some time to come. Our laws are designed to make it expensive to discriminate on illegitimate bases, and with occasional perverse consequences, they often succeed.

God's law is very similar in that there is zero tolerance for prejudice. We all stand equally before God, He views each of us as His children, and we are to view each other likewise. Take a look at just a few of the verses instructing us to "do nothing out of favoritism" (1 Tim. 5:21) because "God does not show favoritism" (Rom. 2:11; Acts 10:34):

- *Impartiality toward others is rooted in one of the greatest commandments:*

    If you really keep the royal law found in Scripture, "Love your neighbor as yourself," you are doing right. But if you show favoritism, you sin and are convicted by the law *(James 2:8-9).*

- *Do not discriminate based on religious beliefs:*

    For there is no difference between Jew and Gentile—the same Lord is Lord of all *(Rom. 10:12).*

- *Do not discriminate against employees:*

    And masters, treat your slaves in the same way. Do not threaten them, since you know that he who is both their Master and yours is in heaven, and there is no favoritism with him *(Eph. 6:9).*

- *Do not discriminate against the poor:*

    My brothers, as believers in our glorious Lord Jesus Christ, don't show favoritism. Suppose a man comes into your meeting wearing a gold ring and fine clothes, and a poor man in shabby clothes also comes in. If you show special attention to the man wearing fine clothes . . . have you not discriminated among yourselves and become judges with evil thoughts? *(James 2:1-4).*

God does not play favorites; who are we to do otherwise? Our job as bosses, easy for some and challenging for others, is to view all applicants and employees as God views them: the same regardless of color, sex, religion, class, disability, and so on. Each is dignified, created in the image of God, and therefore worthy of respectful treatment.

Accordingly, in practice, the Christian boss owes subordinates a work environment free from discrimination and harassment and owes it to the shareholders to keep the company out of court. The design and proper administration of a nondiscrimination policy should therefore be a top priority.

Here are a few brief thoughts on implementing this principle in the workplace:

1. Examine your nondiscrimination policy, and if it is in your power to amend it, be sure that it makes clear that no discrimination or harassment of any kind will be tolerated.
2. Disseminate this policy to all of your subordinates along with the internal procedures for complaints.

3. To minimize lawsuits, be sure that the grievance procedure is clear, fair, and expeditious.
4. Complaints should be investigated promptly, and any violations must be remedied immediately and effectively.
5. Periodic managerial training on these issues is also a good idea (it's actually mandated in some jurisdictions for things such as sexual harassment) because it often eliminates problems before they start and it signals that you are indeed serious about nondiscrimination.

Layoffs and Termination

The question is often posed, "Is it scriptural to fire someone?" For discussion purposes, let's first draw a distinction between firing employees "for cause" and permanently laying them off because of economic pressures. In both cases, I would suggest that the short answer to this question is, "Yes, but . . . ," with the "but" entailing a particular obligation on the part of the Christian boss.

Consider a situation where someone you recently hired simply does not seem to be capable of performing the job adequately. In fact, let's say this person lost two long-term clients because of mistakes in the first few months on the job. Retaining this person is costing you money, and higher-ups are calling for a full explanation. Moreover, without some quick remedial action, they may soon be calling for the head of whoever hired this person. Is it scriptural to let him or her go?

Larry Burkett, founder of Christian Financial Concepts and author of the widely acclaimed work, *Business by the Book*,[8] does an exceptional job with this question. He advises that although the Bible does not prohibit terminating employees, it does compel the Christian boss to ensure before someone is fired that the employee's failures are not a function of poor management. In other words, if, for example, the employee did not know what was expected or if the employee was unaware that he or she was operating incorrectly, it would be wrong to fire him or her.

Burkett's reading of Scripture and institutional knowledge of business have led him to conclude that the following five prerequisites to firing someone should help guard against such improper terminations:

1. Have a clearly defined job description.
2. Have a clearly defined set of job standards: time, dress, expected output, and so on.
3. Communicate your expectations clearly.
4. Communicate your dissatisfaction clearly and quickly.
5. Have a trial correction period.

According to Burkett, given that these prerequisites are met, there are a few biblically justifiable reasons for termination: (1) dishonesty/theft, (2) disobedience/undermining the authority of supervisor, and (3) slothfulness. However, firing someone for "incompetence" is only legitimate if we first determine whether we have simply "misplaced" this employee. That is, to return to our example of the employee who lost two long-term clients, if the employee never had the skill to maintain those accounts but was given that responsibility anyway, the person assigning that work is at fault. If this were the case, our responsibility to this employee, as a Christian boss, would be to locate a job (either within or outside of the organization) that is aligned with his or her current skill set or, alternatively, to upgrade that skill set through training so that the employee can do the present job competently.

The bottom line in all of this is that any action taken against an employee must be done in a spirit of love and concern for all involved. Sometimes that will entail termination (employees who steal, for example, must see that their behavior has consequences if they are ever to change their ways, and shareholders are not properly served by retaining criminals as employees). Often, though, it will not. Before taking this drastic step, the Christian boss should identify whether the root cause of the problem is a lapse of management. Christ did not blame the lost sheep for the erroneous guidance of their earthly shepherds, the Pharisees. He would not blame an employee for the mistakes of management.

Now what about terminating employees for no reason other than economics? We know this happens often: layoffs have been in the news quite a bit in the 1990s. Although the media may blow some of the trend out of proportion, the government statistics are real. According to the U.S. Bureau of Labor Statistics, which began reporting such data in 1995, the number of "mass layoffs" (layoffs of 50 or more employees regardless of duration) by quarter is as follows:

Quarter	Mass Layoffs	Employees Affected
2nd '95	1,412	300,280
3rd '95	2,792	290,513
4th '95	4,308	449,286
1st '96	3,682	381,499
2nd '96	2,868	268,045
3rd '96	2,952	316,870
4th '96	4,529	465,304
1st '97	3,624	355,191
2nd '97	3,178	325,361

Why does clear-cutting of people occur in American business? The American Management Association reports that the rationale for downsizing is typically increased profits and efficiency. Some of their most recent data indicates that 50.6 percent of firms that downsized between 1989 and 1994 soon thereafter realized higher profits.[10] In other words, in just over half of the cases during this time, layoffs may indeed have been a profitable strategy.

But contrary to the simplistic analysis of this trend by many civic, labor, religious, and political leaders, this issue is not so black-and-white as "profits at the expense of people." Without some pruning, the tree will not flourish. And if the tree doesn't bloom well, fewer people will be able to eat of its fruits. Eventually, without preemptive attention, the tree may cease to exist altogether. Downsizing is indeed, in many cases, a survival tactic and/or a means to continued profitability. And it is a tool that has unfortunately become necessary (albeit sometimes overused and exploited) in a world of intense domestic and global competition. So how do we reconcile this "greater good" theory of layoffs with the tremendous individual cost to the millions who have been downsized out of a job recently? What is the role of the servant-leader in this no-win situation?

When considering downsizing to enhance the long-run financial performance of an organization, the servant-leader must vigilantly minimize the cost to the individuals who lose their jobs. Therefore, *before you cut people, you must first exhaust all alternatives to layoff and then, if people still must be cut, do so in a way that preserves their dignity and is sensitive to their family needs.*

To apply this, consider the following options:

- We cut people to save money and to improve efficiency. To meet these same ends, firms are increasingly using "job sharing" arrangements where two or more people essentially share one job. One works from, say, 8:30 to 12:30, and the other from 12:30 to 4:30. Permanent part-time arrangements operate in much the same way, but people do not share jobs. In both cases, though, rather than cutting an individual altogether, a job remains available, but for fewer hours, until that individual finds full-time employment. The burden is essentially carried by two people for a short time rather than being borne entirely by one.

- Since it can be devastating to be involuntarily thrust into the job market when one is in his or her 50s or 60s, partial or phased retirement may be appropriate for older employees. Partial retirement is a permanent part-time arrangement, whereas in a phased retirement scheme, one gradually cuts back hours to zero over months or years. Buyouts and early, no-penalty access to pension plans may also be viable alternatives.

- Earlier in this chapter, we considered what Mark could do with respect to the underperforming single mother in his department. One possible solution that falls in the intersection of profit and Scripture, we said, was to terminate her only after she found an equivalent position somewhere else. Regardless of whether or not it is an official policy of the organization, the Christian boss should do all that he or she can to retain subordinates until they can make a relatively seamless transition to another job.

- Seek suggestions from the employees themselves. They know their situation and their needs better than you do, so they might craft win-win solutions that may have never crossed your mind. Maybe some employees that you would have retained were actually looking to leave and would accept a modest severance to go. Maybe a whole department, in an extreme case, would be willing to take a temporary salary cut to preserve the jobs of all. By soliciting input from those affected, you may be able to reach an optimal resolution.

Christianity teaches that people are more important than profits. That is indisputable. What is significantly less clear is the propriety of cutting hundreds, even thousands of people, to ultimately save the jobs of many more. The intricate task of the Christian boss when contemplating or implementing layoffs is to do more than think strategically. One must think compassionately, never losing sight of the individuals and their families whose lives are disrupted, sometimes destroyed, by this decision. Relegating them to a faceless line on a spreadsheet and then making oneself feel better by tossing them a month's severance does not, I would contend, satisfy the mandates of Scripture. To apply Christianity in a layoff situation is to ensure that those who take the axe for their coworkers' sakes receive proper recognition and care, even though it may be more cost-effective to do otherwise.

Conclusion

If there's one thing that should be clear from this chapter, it is this: *managing people from a Christian perspective takes courage.* One must have the courage to make unconventional decisions and then defend those decisions undaunted before higher-ups. One must resist the temptation to serve one's ego and instead humbly serve one's subordinates. One must have the fortitude to spend an inordinate amount of time implementing solutions that satisfy both the Lord and shareholders. And one must stand firm in one's Christian convictions in those instances where no intersection seems to exist.

The Bible is not just another business resource among many on our bookshelf. It is the Lord's divine policy manual, a free gift to guide the Christian manager in righteous decision making. For the intrepid individual who undertakes this crusade, the payoff is *enormous.* Not only will this person win the "Boss of the Year" award annually and have the most productive department in the organization, but also he or she can enjoy a fulfillment that comes only from doing the Lord's will.

Appendix, Chapter 7
The ServiceMaster Company:
In the Chairman's Own Words

For even the most committed Christians in the marketplace, it is difficult to believe a business can turn a profit while continually constrained by Christian principles. On a more micro level, any Christian boss who is overwhelmed by production deadlines, budget restrictions, pointless meetings, endless paperwork, and continuous pressure to ratchet up performance would likely view things like servant-leadership as another faddish time drain with no proven results. Where is the evidence that in today's business environment one can realistically run a business to the glory of God, be a servant-leader, and still survive?

The evidence exists in Illinois. But it's not just a story of survival; it's a story of industry dominance.

ServiceMaster's Mission

ServiceMaster is an outsourcer for facilities management. Under brand names like Terminix, Tru-Green, ChemLawn, ServiceMaster, Merry Maids, and American Home Shield, they take care of lawns, bugs, broken appliances, furniture repair, carpet and window cleaning, hospitals, schools, food service, long-term care facilities, home health-care agencies, and home inspection. The company traces its roots to a man named Marion Wade, who in 1929 started a moth-proofing company in Chicago. Mr. Wade was not only an astute businessperson but also a devout Christian who sought to apply his faith daily. According to ServiceMaster's web site,

> Marion Wade had a strong personal faith and a desire to honor God in all he did. Translating this into the marketplace, he viewed each individual employee and customer as being made in God's image—worthy of dignity and respect.

Today, those convictions are manifest in four corporate objectives whose import is best described by C. William Pollard, chairman of ServiceMaster, in his book *The Soul of the Firm*[11]:

> When you walk into the lobby of our headquarters in

Downers Grove, Illinois, you see on your right a curving marble wall that stretches ninety feet and stands eighteen feet tall. Carved prominently in the stone of that wall in letters nearly a foot high are four statements that constitute the objectives of our company:

To honor God in all we do

To help people develop

To pursue excellence

To grow profitably

If you were to tour the rest of the building, you would notice that nearly all the workspaces are movable. Most of the walls do not reach the ceiling. Practically everything in the building is changeable and adaptable, just like the marketplace we serve, with its changing demands and opportunities. But the marble wall conveys a permanency that does not change. The principles carved in this stone are lasting.

The first two objectives are end goals. The second two are means goals. As we seek to implement these objectives in the operation of our business, they provide us with a reference point for seeking to do that which is right and avoiding that which is wrong. (Pp. 18-19)

This is, to say the least, a radical approach to business. Glory of God and the development of people are the ends, with the pursuit of excellence and profitability conceived as the vehicles to reach those ends. First and foremost, the ServiceMaster Company exists to honor the Lord.

And if that sometimes conflicts with the profit motive? Pollard says of the tensions between end and means goals,

Leaders in ServiceMaster do not have the option of saying, "Today I am going to honor God and not make a profit," or "Today I am going to make money, and I don't care about developing people." They are continually challenged to make decisions for advancing the firm within the framework of these objectives. If the consequences of a decision or proposed action do not fit, then a change of direction should be taken or no decision should be made. (P. 48)

Thus, the task of decision makers at ServiceMaster is to operate in the intersection of these objectives. Compromise of any of them is not an option.

Implementing the Mission through Training

But any organization can create a pious mission statement. In fact, it may even serve as a clever marketing tool given the right target market.

At ServiceMaster, though, they walk the talk with their employees. With the glory of God and the development of people as end points, ServiceMaster's entire people management system is predicated on respect for human dignity. Says Pollard on this point,

> My belief in God is based on my faith and trust in Jesus Christ. . . . [But] whether or not you share my belief or the claim of God as creator, you should examine the reality of the results of ServiceMaster. Regardless of your starting point, the principle that can be embraced by all is the dignity and worth of every person—every worker. It becomes a living principle as the mission of the firm is understood to include the personal development and growth of that worker. (P. 21)

Personal development and growth implies training, and herein lies the implementation secret to ServiceMaster's success. They give employees skills, they give them knowledge, they empower them and bring meaning to their work lives. Whether they be janitors, window washers, lawn cutters, or managers, ServiceMaster pays tremendous attention to their development.

To illustrate, consider this excerpt from *Why America Doesn't Work* by Chuck Colson and Jack Eckerd. ServiceMaster's former CEO Ken Wessner was on-site to consummate a contract with a new client, a municipal hospital. To the puzzlement of the hospital's chief of staff, Dr. Underwood, Wessner requested to meet with the doctors, nurses, and technicians before he met with the maintenance staff:

> "Ours is a very complicated business that appears deceptively simple," Wessner began as he addressed the group. "Some may regard the cleaning business as menial and beneath them. But at ServiceMaster, the housekeeper, window washer, or floor finisher is just as important as the Ph.D. we employ to research and develop products. We begin each new contract with the belief that every individual's work is valuable and dignifying. That's why we try to

maintain the current staff. It's also why I asked to meet with you today before I meet with the staff."

Curious glances ricocheted around the table until a surgeon broke the silence. "What do we have to do with how you clean the buildings?"

"Well, you will help us train," Wessner said. "We have put a great deal of thought into our training programs. We want our employees' lives enriched by what they do each day. To do that, we need your help."

"I don't think my colleagues understand what it is we are to do," said Dr. Underwood.

"Each month we hold Housekeeping Councils for our employees. This is a thirty to forty-five minute training session where every employee is briefed on various aspects of hospital operations. For example, I hear you have some new radiology equipment here. We would ask one of you to come in and explain how the equipment is used generally, who it helps, and how it helps them."

"Do you expect janitors to understand radiology?" asked one of the radiologists.

"No, but we do expect them to be able to see the vital part they play in the mission of the hospital and its various functions. It connects them to a greater goal and inspires commitment to quality, cleanliness, and even those of you on the professional staff."[12]

Echoing this philosophy, Chairman Pollard writes: "People want to work for a cause, not just a living" (p. 45). It builds self-esteem and purpose. However, demonstrating to an employee the connection between his or her work and some broader organizational objective does more than just enhance individual self-worth. It also boosts productivity, customer service, and ultimately profit. The nexus is explained in Pollard's chapter titled "Productivity as a Virtue":

If a worker understands the task *and* how it fits within the mission and purpose of the firm, he can also be expected to respond in a positive way to the unexpected. It is this potential that is unique to a person and not possible with a machine. When the unexpected happens, the worker not only meets the standard, but exceeds the expectation of the customer. . . .

[Faculty] at the Harvard Business School have done extensive research on various service firms, including ServiceMaster. Their studies clearly indicate that customer satisfaction is directly related to quick response in solving problems. Mistakes will happen, but when the service provider is trained, motivated, and enabled to correct the mistake on the spot, the customer usually will view the problem and its resolution as a job well done. (Pp. 81-83)

"The challenge for every firm, especially a service company," Pollard concludes, "is . . . to empower the person who deals directly with the customer." Empowerment does more than dignify the employee. It is, when coupled with appropriate training and employee commitment to the organization, an effective strategy to satisfy customers and to grow the business.

Cultivating Servant-Leadership

Beyond training and empowerment of rank-and-file employees, ServiceMaster uses an unconventional approach to management training that facilitates both employee dignity and servanthood among leaders. To ensure that bosses appreciate the daily tribulations inherent in their subordinates' jobs, it is ServiceMaster's policy that bosses occasionally perform this work for themselves. These are what ServiceMaster calls "We Serve" days, and they are considered extremely valuable by the firm. Notes Pollard:

Good training seeks to understand how people feel about their work and about themselves and about their contribution to the well-being of those they serve. For example, if you are involved in management, then part of your training should include an experience to see what it is like to do the hands-on work and to feel the exertions of those you are going to manage. That is why we require every manager to spend some time actually doing the task that he will ultimately manage. And it is for the same reason that every employee at ServiceMaster, regardless of position, spends at least one day per year working in the field, providing one of our services to the customer. (P. 54)

Pollard offers several anecdotes to illustrate the value of this training technique, two of which are replicated here. In the first, Pollard tells of his initial days as a senior vice president at

ServiceMaster as he worked with a housekeeping team at a hospital. The second example recounts the story of a young employee, Dave Aldridge, who had been recruited to work for ServiceMaster right out of grad school.

One incident that took place during the first few months of my training is still a vivid reminder to me of how others often treat and view those who serve in routine assignments. I was working on a busy corridor of the hospital. I had just set out my wet-floor signs and was about to mop the floor . . . when suddenly a lady stopped and asked, "Aren't you Bill Pollard?" I responded that I was, and she identified herself as a distant relative of my wife. She looked at me and my mop, shook her head, and asked, "Aren't you a lawyer?" as if to say "Can't you get a better job?" I paused, looked down at my bucket, and said, "No, I have a new job." By this time, several other people had gathered around. She was now embarrassed and leaned close to me and whispered, "Is everything all right at home?" (Pp. 14-15)

Dave Aldridge . . . tells about one of his "We Serve" experiences in a hospital:

The hospital was opening a new wing, and I was helping to prepare the birthing suites. I was on my hands and knees cleaning baseboards. An excited group of nurses who would be serving in this new area walked through. As they walked by, I looked up and said hello, and no one responded. I wanted to cry out, "Hey, I have an MBA and my wife is a nurse!" But the reality was that no one cared or thought I was worth acknowledging. (P. 56)

"We Serve" days engender a managerial appreciation for the plight of subordinates that is central to cultivating servant-leaders throughout the organization. Pollard, not surprisingly, credits the gospel as the original source of such ideas:

In John 13 we read the story of how Jesus took a towel and a basin of water and washed the disciples' feet. In doing so, He taught His disciples that no leader is greater than the people he leads, and that even the humblest task is worthy for a leader to do.

Does this example fit in today's world, two thousand years later? There certainly is no scarcity of feet to wash, and towels are always available. I suggest the only limitation, if there is one, involves the ability of each of us as leaders to be on our own hands and knees, to compromise our pride, to be involved, and to have compassion for those we serve.

For people to grow and develop within a firm, its leaders and managers must be prepared to serve as part of their leadership. Servant-leadership is part of our ethic, and it means that the leaders in our firm should never ask anyone to do anything that they are unwilling to do for themselves. (P. 130)

Furthermore, applying this to compensation, the strategies of pay-for-performance, profit sharing, and employee stock ownership are all conceived as part and parcel of servanthood:

The leader who serves and believes in people is also responsible for fair compensation or distribution of results. How do you compensate and pay people for what they produce? . . . The ServiceMaster plan seeks to pay based on performance and promote based on potential. We believe that those responsible for producing profits should share in those profits, and those who produce more should share more. . . . Over the past twenty years, the incentives and profit sharing paid by ServiceMaster to its people have averaged 45 to 50 percent of incremental growth in earnings. The people producing the results have shared in the results as they have also contributed to the growth of the firm. They have also shared in the ownership of the firm. More than 20 percent of ServiceMaster is now owned by the employees who are making it happen. (Pp. 131-32)

Financial Performance without Compromising Christian Principles

Now what about that bottom line? The results of this corporate philosophy speak for themselves: ServiceMaster currently operates in more than 30 countries on five continents, serving over 6 million customers. It is the United States' leading provider of outsourcing for facilities management and currently boasts a systemwide revenue *in excess of 4 billion dollars a year.* And according to its chairman, it all starts with running the business to glorify God. Honoring God means respecting the dignity of the person. That respect implicates training to build employee skills, to empower them, and to bring meaning to their work. These more skilled, more motivated employees who are empowered to think independently tend to exceed customers' expectations, and this translates into growth of both the customer base and the bottom line.

"God and business do mix," asserts Pollard with a knowing confidence. "For us, the common link between God and profit is people."

8

Taking the First Critical Step

*S*IOWLY LEANING BACK *in his desk chair, Mark silently sent up a quick prayer for guidance. In the 25 years since he first walked through the stately double doors of the firm, he had gained increasing discernment about living the Christian faith in the secular workplace. But it would take more than accumulated knowledge to properly counsel this man who stood at a crucial crossroad. He needed divine direction—and soon.*

Before him sat a young, dejected manager who six months earlier had been caught skimming funds from one of the firm's operating accounts. Divorced, drowning in debt, and religiously confused, Brett at that point had sought life advice—and a second chance—from Mark, a man whose integrity and professional acumen he respected immensely. In light of Brett's repentant attitude, Mark indeed gave him that chance but also took the opportunity to share with Brett, whom he knew to be a nominal Christian, the secret to his quarter century of business success: the gospel.

Brett had long felt a need to make his faith more central in his life, and clearly his life was offtrack, so he was receptive to the message. In fact, he seemed to hang on Mark's every word, he asked a lot of relevant questions, and shortly thereafter, sensing a tremendous weight being lifted, he enthusiastically vowed to take his Christian faith seriously for the first time in his life.

In the months that followed that pivotal day, Brett frequently visited Mark's office for sage advice regarding a Christian approach to some issue or problem. Moreover, he voraciously read everything he could find about the nature of God, about theology, and about how to implement the doctrinal pillars of the Christian faith. His knowledge of the Bible was rapidly becoming encyclopedic as he invested several hours a day in both Scripture and Christian radio.

But now, a forlorn Brett sat before Mark, guilt-ridden and over-whelmed by frustration. It wasn't working. Even after cramming so many timeless truths into his brain, he still could not live the faith. Granted, he was no longer stealing from the company, but he still disliked most of his coworkers, he still demanded too much of his subordinates, he still found himself enjoying (and retelling) insensitive and off-color jokes, and he was still harboring lustful and prideful thoughts.

Despondent and disillusioned, Brett told Mark that maybe he just wasn't cut out for this Christianity stuff after all.

———·———

Light-years separate knowing what is right from doing what is right. Through sermons, Bible studies, growth groups, books, courses, mentors, and various other avenues, we Christians spend a lifetime pursuing a thorough knowledge of the Truth. Additionally, we spend untold hours on our knees, praying for wisdom, praying for genuine comprehension and retention of scriptural instruction. We download an immense, eternal data set into our memory banks, but then, inexplicably, when the time comes to exercise our faith, we often fall far short of God's will. Whether at work or at home, in a crowd or in solitude, among friends, strangers, or foes, for some reason we drop the blessed ball. As with Brett, we learn that our knowledge of the Truth is insufficient to transform us.

If you are among the legions of people who have faltered repeatedly when attempting to apply the Christian faith, take heart. You're in good company! In one of the most striking passages of the New Testament (translated, I think, most clearly in the New Living Translation), the apostle Paul confesses this very same deficiency:

> I don't understand myself at all, for I really want to do what is right, but I don't do it. Instead, I do the very thing I hate. I know perfectly well that what I am doing is wrong. . . . but I can't help myself, because it is the sin inside me that makes me do these evil things.
>
> I know I am rotten through and through so far as my old sinful nature is concerned. No matter which way I turn, I can't make myself do right. I want to, but I can't. When I want to do good, I don't. And when I try not to do wrong, I do it anyway. . . . Oh, what a miserable person I am! *(Rom. 7:15-19, 24).*

That's pretty arresting language. Here we have the Lord's chosen messenger to the Gentiles, the one He selected to write at least 13 books of the New Testament, admitting that even he cannot dependably do what is right. Now, 2,000 years later, it's our turn to echo this lamentation—especially in our workplace.

We can read some book on applying Christianity on the job and get all fired up to be salt and light and to really let our colleagues and customers see Christ through us. We can gain all sorts of book knowledge about scriptural principles and even devise clever ways to explain them, just in case someone asks us about our faith. We can convince ourselves that we're ready for anything, that we've got all the ecclesiastical bases covered. And then, out of nowhere, the noxious combination of corporate culture and our sinful nature overcomes us, mercilessly undermining our most sincere efforts. We tried to walk like Christ and quickly stumbled. Then we immediately felt guilty, asked for forgiveness, and tried again. And then stumbled again! Eventually, it's natural to become so frustrated by this iterative, seemingly fruitless process that we simply throw up our arms and chuck the whole venture. "It's futile," we reason. "I'll never have the power to do this right."

If, in fact, you were to say that, you'd be exactly right. On your own, you will never have this power. If you approach this endeavor as you might any other project at work—relying exclusively on your skills, your talents, your energy, and even your spiritually mature coworkers to achieve the desired ends —you're setting yourself up for disappointment. No matter how hard you work, no matter how much you know, no matter how committed you are to change, and no matter how wise your well-intentioned advisers, you will not be able to pursue this calling for very long—much less for an entire career—without tapping into the limitless power of God through His Holy Spirit.

Pastor Tony Evans in his book *The Promise* offers an extended, brilliant illustration of this point. He opens this study of the Holy Spirit with a hypothetical situation:

> You have just been to the store and seen the most incredible refrigerator you can imagine. The thing is huge. It not only has all the bells and whistles you expect, it has some you've never seen before. This refrigerator will do

everything but turn the lights off, put the dog out, and lock up at night. It costs thousands more than a normal refrigerator, but you buy it anyway because it is unbelievable.

The store delivers your new refrigerator to you home. In your excitement, you shop for all the goodies you want to store in it. You stock that refrigerator with everything you can think of, then retire for the evening.

The next morning you run into the kitchen excitedly, only to discover that the milk is spoiled, the ice cream is running out the bottom of the freezer compartment, and the vegetables are changing color. Your new refrigerator is not working.

You call the store to give the people there a piece of your Christian mind. The man says, "I don't understand it. Open the door and see if the light comes on." You open the door. No light.

"Put your ear up close to the refrigerator and tell me if you can hear the hum of the motor." You do, and there's no hum.

He then says, "There's a cord in the back of your refrigerator. Please check to see whether it has been plugged in." Lo and behold, you go to the back of your new refrigerator and there it is. The cord has not been plugged in.

. . . Now that's a long way around to state an obvious truth. No matter how much you paid for it, your refrigerator won't work the way it was designed to work unless it is plugged in to electric power. Neither will your spiritual life work unless you are plugged in to Holy Ghost power.

When God saved us, He gave us all the component parts necessary for spiritual life and victory. But we are dependent creatures. We have not been designed to work on our own. Only as we are empowered by the indwelling of the Holy Spirit will we produce what our lives are supposed to produce. If you don't rely on that power, don't be surprised if the milk of your life turns sour and the ice cream begins to melt.[1]

From here, Dr. Evans dispenses more than 350 pages of incisive instruction about the presence, purpose, and provision of this mysterious Third Person of the Trinity. Clearly, this is an intricate subject whose parameters are beyond our scope here.

But, as this illustration poignantly reveals, our need for the Counselor is a basic one: *we cannot consistently succeed in living the Christian life without the Holy Spirit's supernatural assistance.* Therefore, if we neglect to plug into this power source when attempting to apply the faith at work, we are likely to become exasperated and eventually abandon the effort.

This was the fatal mistake of our friend Brett, as it is for so many of us stubborn, independently minded folks. We attempt to be self-sufficient and to perform a task that by design we cannot perform alone. We may have the right destination in mind, and we certainly have a divine road map in Scripture, but we rely on a vehicle that could never make the trip: ourselves.

For this reason, *to consistently apply the Christian faith in the workplace, the first critical step is to acknowledge your dependence upon God.* It's simply too hard to apply on your own. Often, it's too inconvenient and costly. There are too many people who will set up roadblocks. And if they don't sabotage the effort, your carnal nature will. Therefore, if you want to live your faith at work for the rest of your life, your willingness to turn your life over to Christ and let Him direct it must come first. It's the prerequisite to empowerment by the Holy Spirit and the key to perpetual victory in the workplace.

And when we are willing to depend wholly on the Lord, to follow Him regardless of the consequences, a miraculous transformation occurs. Our colaborer Paul writes,

> Therefore, I urge you, brothers, in view of God's mercy, to offer your bodies as living sacrifices, holy and pleasing to God—this is your spiritual act of worship. Do not conform any longer to the pattern of this world, but be transformed by the renewing of your mind *(Rom. 12:1-2).*

After we offer ourselves as "living sacrifices"—after we vow to serve Him unconditionally—our minds will be renewed. That is, the way we think about *everything* will change. On the job, our attitude toward our peers, our boss, our subordinates, our customers, and everyone else will become more like Christ's, more like that of a servant. We will also find ourselves with the ability to resolve conflicts in a way that is pleasing to the Lord, and our capacity to forgive mistreatment and personal attacks will be virtually unlimited. We will at long last discover the courage to witness when the occasion presents itself. And less encumbered by pride, ambition, and greed, we will more readily strike an appropriate balance between our work and our family lives. Overall, we will begin to conceive everything that we do at work as an opportunity to glorify God, acknowledging Him as our ultimate CEO. This is the essence of what it means to live the Christian faith in the workplace, and it all begins when we agree to become God's property and allow Him to change the way we think.

This implies that each one of us has been blessed with the privilege to make a choice. Each of us has the option—today—to set this transformational process in motion by devoting his or her life to God's service. We each have the option—today—to promise the Lord that no matter what, we'll do things His way rather than our own way.

By far, this is the most important decision you'll ever make, in or out of the workplace. And the good news is that no one can prevent you from saying yes to the Lord. By the grace of God, this is a decision that resides entirely with you.

NOTES

Chapter 1

1. Glenda Beasley v. Health Care Services Corp., 940 F.2d. 1085 (7th Cir., 1991).
2. Wilson v. US West Communications, 860 F.Supp. 665 (8th Cir., 1995).
3. Ned N. Cary V. Anheuser-Busch, Inc., 741 F.Supp. 1219 (E.D. Vir., 1988).
4. Ruth Kolodiej v. Warren Smith, 588 N.E. 2d. 634 (Mass., 1992).
5. Isaiah Brown v. Polk County, Iowa, 61 F.3d. 650 (8th Cir., 1995).
6. Robert L. Vernon v. City of Los Angeles, 27 R.3d. 1385 (9th Cir., 1994).

Chapter 2

1. Gerry Spence, *How to Argue and Win Every Time* (New York: St. Martin's Press, 1996).
2. Roger Fisher and William Ury, *Getting to Yes: Negotiating Agreement Without Giving In* (New York: Penguin Books, 1981).
3. C. Michael Donaldson and Mimi Donaldson, *Negotiating for Dummies* (New York: IDG Press Worldwide, 1996).
4. See Ray Stedman's sermon titled "The Cure for Conflict," reproduced on Peninsula Bible Church's Stedman Archive on the Internet at http://www.pbc.org/dp/stedman/ephesians/0130.html.
5. Donna Eder and Janet Lynne Enke, "The Structure of Gossip: Opportunities and Constraints on the Collective Expression Among Adolescents," *American Sociological Review* (1991), 56:494-508.

Chapter 3

1. Bill Hybels and Mark Mittenberg, *Becoming a Contagious Christian* (Grand Rapids: Zondervan, 1994).
2. Michael Green and Alister McGrath, *How Shall We Reach Them? Defending and Communicating the Christian Faith to Non-Believers* (Nashville: Thomas Nelson, 1995).
3. Josh McDowell, *Evidence That Demands a Verdict*, Vols. I and II (Nashville: Thomas Nelson, 1979).
4. F. F. Bruce, *The New Testament Documents: Are They Reliable?* (Downers Grove, Ill.: InterVarsity Press, 1964).
5. Christian Answers Network, 1944 North Gilbert Rd., Gilbert, AZ 85234-3304.
6. Nelson Glueck, *Rivers in the Desert: History of Negev* (Philadelphia: Jewish Publications Society of America, 1969), 31.

Chapter 4

1. Michael Reinemer, "Work Happy," *American Demographics* (July 1995): 26-31.

Chapter 5

1. Les Carter and Frank Minirth, *The Anger Workbook* (Nashville: Thomas Nelson, 1993).

2. Ibid., 24-39.

3. *Daily Labor Report*, "Statement of EeOC Chairman Casellas Before the Senate Labor and Human Resources Committee" (Washington, D.C.: Bureau of National Affairs, May 24, 1995).

4. Fisher and Ury, *Getting to Yes.*

Chapter 6

1. See Keith Epstein, "How We Countered the 'Family-time' Famine," *The Washington Post,* April 11, 1994.

2. James T. Bond, Dana Friedman, and Ellen Galinsky, *The Changing Workforce* (Families and Work Institute, 1993), 75.

3. Family Research Council, *In Focus,* on the Internet at http://www.townhall.com/frc/infocus/IF95L7FT.html.

4. Donald Merideth, *Becoming One* (Nashville: Thomas Nelson, 1991).

5. See, for example, *Publish Heath Reports,* "Divorce Update" 110 (July/August 1995): 507.

6. William Cosby, *Fatherhood* (New York: Doubleday, 1986), 158.

7. From *Dr. Dobson Answers Your Questions About Raising Children* by Dr. James Dobson © 1982, 13-14. Used by permission of Tyndale House Publishers, Inc. All rights reserved.

8. Gary Smalley and John Trent, *Love Is a Decision* (Dallas: Word, 1989), 25. All rights reserved.

9. Billy Graham, *Answers to Life's Problems* (Dallas: Word, 1988), 42-43. All rights reserved.

Chapter 7

1. Max DePree, *Leadership Is an Art* (New York: Dell, 1990).

2. See, for example, Mark A. Huselid, "The Impact of Human Resource Management Practices on Turnover, Productivity, and Corporate Financial Performance," *Academy of Management Journal,* 38:3 (1995): 635-72.

3. Richard Mahue, "Introductions, Illustrations, and Conclusions" in *Expository Preaching: Balancing the Science and Art of Biblical Exposition,* ed. John MacArthur (Dallas: Word, 1992), 242-54.

4. Douglas Kruse, *Profit Sharing: Does It Make a Difference?* (Kalamazoo, Mich.: Upjohn Institute, 1993).

5. Society for Human Resource Management, *Work and Family Survey* (Washington, D.C.: SHRM, 1997). A synopsis of these findings can be found on the Internet at http://www.shrm.org/press/release/wrkfam.htm.

6. *Daily Labor Report,* "Study Finds Better Pay, Satisfaction for Telecommuters, Self-Employed," Bureau of National Affairs: Washington, D.C., June 23, 1993; see also Robert E. Calem, "Working at Home for Better or Worse," *The New York Times,* April 18, 1993, C2.

7. Society for Human Resource Management, *Work and Family Survey.*

8. Larry Burkett, *Business By the Book: The Complete Guide of Biblical Principles for Business Men and Women* (Nashville: Thomas Nelson, 1990), 104-25.

9. This information is available on the Bureau of Labor Statistics web site: http://stats.bls.gov.

10. *Daily Labor Report,* "Survey Shows Latest Round of Downsizing Aimed at Boosting Efficiency, Profits," Bureau of National Affairs: Washington, D.C., September 28, 1994.

11. Taken from *The Soul of the Firm* by C. William Pollard. Copyright © 1996 by ServiceMaster Foundation. Used by permission of Zondervan Publishing House.

12. Chuck Colson and Jack Eckerd, *Why America Doesn't Work* (Dallas: Word, 1996), 157-58. All rights reserved.

Chapter 8

1. Tony Evans, *The Promise* (Dallas: Word, 1996), 3-4. All rights reserved.